Patricia O'Brien King

Deseret Book Company
Salt Lake City, Utah

©1983 Deseret Book Company
All rights reserved
Printed in the United States of America

First printing January 1983
Second printing August 1983
Third printing March 1984

Library of Congress Cataloging in Publication Data
King, Patricia O'Brien.
    Solo: the miraculous story of a woman who refused
to give up.
    1. Survival (after airplane accidents, shipwrecks, etc.)
2. Aeronautics—Accidents—1981.   3.   Jaussi, Sherleen.
I. Title.
TL553.9.K56   1983   363.1'2481'0924   [B]   82-23483
ISBN 0-87747-965-8

This book is dedicated to all those whose untiring efforts on the ground and in the air made this story possible. The prayers and concern of people from all walks of life and from many different faiths were a strong and meaningful factor as the events retold here unfolded.

Two Civil Air Patrol pilots, Kay N. Ahlstrom and Harold F. Steab, were killed in an accident after the search had concluded. After stopping at an airshow en route to their homes and then refueling for the completion of their trip, they crashed on takeoff. Both died instantly. They were among the many who were willing to risk their lives in an air search.

"Greater love hath no man than this, that a man lay down his life for his friends." (John 15:13.)

Tuesday, June 23, 1981

1

It was that time in the morning when it seems as though all the rest of the world is still asleep. Alone with her thoughts as she dressed quietly, Sherleen Jaussi knew that wasn't really true. Her husband, Jim, was often at the hospital at this hour delivering a baby, a place as busy right now as it had been all night. The coal miners in the community, as well as those who worked for Utah Power and Light, left for work by 6:15, so their neighbor Brent Johnson would be getting ready to go to work. Craig Humes would be up and preparing to meet her at the airport in a few minutes, and much of Price would be doing early-morning things right on schedule, but doing them quietly so that children and others who didn't have to be awake yet would not be disturbed.

With the longest day of the year only forty-eight hours behind them, the Jaussi children were still deep in the sweet, heavy sleep of those whose busy playtime the night before had gone far into the evening hours.

How I would love to stay here with them this morning—have some fun with them, thought Sherleen. *But then, I think just about anything would be more fun than that lonely plane ride right now. I wish I had talked Craig out of this cross-country solo today. I just hate to be up in that airplane alone. Why did I ever start this?* But even as she pulled the peach-colored velour shirt over her head, Sherleen reviewed why she had chosen to take flying lessons.

The decision she and Jim had made ten months earlier to move their family and his obstetrical practice from Salt Lake City to Price, Utah, had been a very difficult one. An opportunity to join with his old friend, Dr. Lynn Dayton, in a large and well-organized practice was not enough to make moving that far away from their two mothers any less painful. Sherleen's mother lived in Georgetown, Idaho, and the concern Sherleen felt at not being able to get back and forth quickly and easily to visit and help her weighed heavily on their minds. Nor could many day-long automobile trips between the two cities be considered, with their own five children needing their care and attention. Flying seemed an ideal solution, and only after much thought and prayer had the couple begun their instruction. The logic of their decision wasn't any comfort this morning, however, as Sherleen forced herself back to the present and hurried toward the front door.

Glasses—go back and get your glasses, she thought to herself, though it seemed a little silly, since she would be gone only a few hours, and her contacts should work fine for that long.

Deanna Humes had driven out to Carbon County airport with her husband, Craig. After carefully going over her flight plan with her instructor, Sherleen asked, "Deanna, why don't you hop in and ride with me this morning? I know I can't count it as a cross-country, but it would still be good practice, and I'd just love to have you along."

"Sherleen," Craig interrupted before his wife could respond, "you've done everything you need to do to prepare for this—all your ground school and almost three times as many hours in the air with me as you have to have before going alone. We've covered everything you need to know many times. You have to go sometime."

Sherleen's first cross-country had not been at all unpleasant. Craig had followed behind in the Cherokee with the whole Jaussi family aboard, and the flight had culminated at Bear Lake for a Memorial Day picnic, an event they had all enjoyed.

Sherleen had not enjoyed the second solo, however, to Hanksville and the Canyonlands. The other airplane hadn't accompanied her that time, and she had felt uncomfortably alone.

The flight this morning was to be a three-legged course charted for Grand Junction, Colorado; Blanding, Utah; then back home to Price. Ten hours of cross-country solo flight were required before Sherleen could obtain her pilot's license. One of those solo flights had to follow a triangular course, with one leg at least one hundred nautical miles in length. Three solo landings at an airport with a control tower were also requirements that would be accomplished on today's trip.

She climbed into the Tomahawk and began her preflight checklist, then stuck her head out the window and announced gleefully, "Guess what—the battery's dead!"

Craig grinned as he answered, "No it isn't. I was the last one to fly it."

"Oh, shucks, I haven't turned the master switch on. Guess I hit the fuel pump switch instead. Well, it was worth a try!"

The student pilot had done everything she could—aside from simply saying "I won't do it"—to get out of going. She had run out of delay tactics.

Sherleen's courage and spunky personality made Craig forget, most of the time, what a slight person she actually was. This morning she seemed especially tiny, barely five feet, four inches tall, her brown wedge-cut hair accenting deep brown eyes. But tiny or not, Craig knew that Sherleen was well-prepared for this solo flight and capable of becoming a fine pilot. So with Craig standing on the runway feeling as though he had just given that slight shove out of the nest to one who must try her wings, Sherleen flew off into the eastern sunrise. It was 6:45 A.M.

2

The round-robin flight plan Sherleen had filed at Price allowed about twenty minutes at each stop to get out of the plane, have someone sign her logbook, and then take off on the next leg. As she flew toward Grand Junction, she began to enjoy her trip, marking off her mapped checkpoints right on schedule. She called into the control tower as she neared Grand Junction, requesting assistance in finding the airport—she'd been there only once before and had approached from another direction. The tower advised her to continue following the highway, which would lead her right into the airport. The wind tossed her about a bit as she came down—not a rough landing, but definitely not one where she just sailed in and put the plane down.

Sherleen popped into Horizon Aviation to find someone to refuel the plane, chatted briefly with some pilots and other people, and in a few minutes was back inside the Tomahawk, ready to head on to Blanding. She taxied out and spoke into the microphone. "This is two-six-zero-niner Delta; I'm a student pilot and I'm ready for clearance to taxi to the active runway." On the way to the runway she passed another airplane.

"Give way to the student pilot," came instructions from the tower, and Sherleen laughed as she saw the plane scoot as far away as possible.

As she approached the active runway, she thought perhaps she had better call in again to make sure that she was cleared.

"Zero-niner Delta to tower, am I cleared to use the active runway?"

"No, zero-niner Delta, you are not cleared to enter the runway. When you are ready, let us know, and we'll clear you."

"This is zero-niner Delta, and I am ready to enter the runway."

"Zero-niner Delta, you are cleared to enter the active runway. Check your density altitude, and have a good day."

"This is zero-niner Delta rolling on one-one. Requesting a right-hand turnout, southwest departure."

"You are cleared, zero-niner Delta, for your departure. Good luck."

Sherleen was not accustomed to Grand Junction's large runway, a necessity because of the commercial jets that fly in and out of there. The takeoff seemed much longer and her climb much slower than she was used to. She concluded that the problem was probably due to air density. But at last she began to gain altitude easily, and she relaxed as she entered the second phase of her journey. For company, she left the radio on the airport frequency and listened to the conversation from the control tower as she looked at the map to find the first of the two checkpoints that would assure her she was on course and was not being affected by wind or other factors.

As the Tomahawk neared the mountains, the Grand Junction tower announced some turbulence in the area. Sherleen glanced over her shoulder toward Grand Junction and noticed that she could still see the airport. In the instant she turned back around, the turbulence she had just been warned about began tossing the plane.

Oh, drat, I hate this stuff.

Craig had told Sherleen to take the mountains at 8,500 feet. Immediately a huge downdraft dropped the plane to only 8,000 feet.

Oh no, it's just like that night—

Only once in all her training had Craig been upset with her. They had been doing touch-and-go practice and had hit a downdraft, ending up only 1,000 feet above the ground. Craig warned her over and over of the three most important things she must remember about flying: airspeed, airspeed, and airspeed. "You're too close to the ground to lose airspeed. You'll go down," he'd said, and Sherleen had started to cry. But she never forgot what a downdraft can do—it can kill people.

Just as Sherleen recovered from the first drop, she felt another, as though a huge hand was pushing the plane steadily down into the trees. A thousand terrible thoughts raced through her mind. She was going to crash. Most people in air crashes were killed. Recovery from the downdraft seemed impossible. Without any warning she was leaving all the things she knew, all the things she was familiar with, all the people she loved. "Please," she cried out, "please don't let me die!"

"Please, *please* don't let me die!"

The Tomahawk was now skimming the tops of the quaking aspens, and its airspeed had slowed to about sixty-seven knots, roughly equivalent to eighty miles per hour. Sherleen looked out over the plane. *It's not hurt badly—if I can just fly it.*

But even as the thought crossed her mind, she knew there was not enough power in the small plane to regain the needed speed and altitude. It began bouncing along the tops of the trees like a balloon on an air bubble.

Craig's warnings came back to her. "If you're going to crash, you've got to keep flying the plane. Take it down as though you're landing it. If you fly the plane to the end, you *can* walk away from it."

Sherleen felt an urge to pull back on the yoke and lift the plane up, but Craig had often warned her that that would cause a stall and pull her into the ground nose first. "Keep your airspeed at all costs," he had drilled into her, so she kept the nose of the plane down, lowering it even more, hitting the trees harder and harder. Suddenly there was no time to think of anything else except flying the plane. Ahead loomed two huge pine trees, only ten feet apart and directly in her path.

You are really going down, Sherleen. You're going to crash. Fly the plane, keep flying the plane.

In the next instant the right wing smacked into a tall aspen tree, breaking both the wing and the aspen and pivoting the plane sideways between the two pine trees. The terrifying sounds made by the fractured wing and severed tree registered briefly in Sherleen's mind as the plane was flung wildly to the ground, upside down. More sounds—this time of china dishes shattering and the windshield breaking—but the thick forest growth had cushioned the fall enough so that the bubble in which she sat was still intact. The china dishes stopped clattering, the branches cracked no more, the engine ceased to rattle. All was suddenly quiet. She opened her eyes and heard herself say, "I'm alive! I'm really alive. Thank you for letting me live."

3

Gratitude welled up within Sherleen, and she wanted to pour out more thanks, but she didn't dare. Thirty-two gallons of gasoline had been pumped into the plane's tanks only fifteen minutes earlier. She had to get out quickly.

She undid her seat belt and lowered herself to the top of the bubble. Her right shoulder was in extreme pain. *You don't have time for a silly broken arm right now,* she thought, as she reached for the mike with her other arm. The mike was dead, but she turned through the frequencies, hoping somehow she'd get a response. The threat of an explosion still nagged at her; the Humes had spoken only that morning of a friend who'd gone down in a crop duster and escaped from the plane just moments before it burst into flames. But she knew she had to make sure the emergency locator transmitter had turned on. The ELT had dropped from its case on impact—a good sign—but she had difficulty as she fumbled at the antenna with hands that were badly cut and swelling rapidly.

In an automatic and trauma-clouded reaction, Sherleen determined she should tidy up the inside of the plane a bit before leaving it to burn. She gathered together some items that had flown out of a cardboard box, rearranged them carefully, then reached for the door to get out. The pilot's side was blocked by a broken wing, and panic swelled within her as she tried the other door and found she was locked in at the top of the bubble, now pushed into the ground. She clawed frantically at the dirt that had been forced into that part of the bubble, released the catch, and pushed until the door opened about a foot and a half. Pulling her purse and jacket after her, she crawled out of the plane, then stood and walked as rapidly as possible to a tree some twenty feet away. It was Sherleen's last walk for six and a half weeks.

At the tree she crumpled to her knees and began pouring out expressions of gratitude to her Father in heaven. His mercy nearly overwhelmed her, and she tried earnestly to communicate to Him how thankful she was that her life had been spared. She prayed for several minutes, then collapsed into an exhausted sleep.

Almost immediately an excruciating pain in her right arm forced her awake. *I can't stand this pain,* Sherleen thought, and in a desperate try to relieve it, she flung the arm as hard as she could. It snapped instantly into place.

With the elimination of one nagging hurt, she became aware of a terrible pain in her leg—she must have turned or pulled a muscle in her groin. She decided she just couldn't dwell on it. Since she was awake, she would take inventory.

Okay, where am I hurt? Blood on her shirt indicated a possible nosebleed, though she didn't recall having one. The real beating had apparently been taken by her arms and legs. The trunk of her body had been strapped securely in position in the plane, while her limbs in those last few seconds must have tossed wildly about in a subconscious effort to catch herself. One knee was badly cut, and her stocking was glued to it with blood. One hand had begun to swell rapidly, and the other had three deep gashes that she was sure Jim would want to sew up. A fingernail had been ripped off—probably the most painful thing of all—and her wedding rings were smashed nearly flat.

Blood and dirt were ground into her face, so Sherleen took one of the two tissues in her purse and worked for several minutes moistening the tissue with saliva and washing as well as she could.

Gradually a new fear set in as halos seemed to form around her eyes, blurring to blue, then red. Again she prayed, knowing how difficult it would be to find her way out if she lost her sight. Fear of blindness soon gave way to an even greater concern—forest fire! She could both hear and smell the steady dripping of gasoline. Maybe if she could stand, she could stay ahead of a fire. But that was impossible—she couldn't put any weight on her injured leg. Even crawling caused intense pain. Several terrifying minutes passed before her panic began to subside. A spark would have to ignite the fumes, and the plane was still resting inertly in its upside-down position.

Forty-five minutes had passed since the crash, and it was now ten o'clock. Though she was anxious to be found immediately, Sherleen realized that she had at least two hours to wait. Her flight plan wasn't supposed to close until around noon. She began making plans for her arrival home, promising herself that before Jim took her to the hospital that afternoon, she would go home and have a nice warm bath and clean off all this blood and dirt and perspiration. In the meantime, since several of her fingernails were broken and cracked, she would file them while she waited.

4

Jim Jaussi left Valley View Medical Building a few minutes after noon and drove home for his usual lunch with Sherleen. As he approached the house, he wondered why the car wasn't there. He hoped all had gone well with Sherleen's flight that morning. The children hadn't heard from her, so he quickly phoned Craig Humes, whose full-time job was as a pediatric assistant. Craig immediately alerted a friend at the Huntington airport, Don Owen, and

Don flew to 13,000 feet to try to contact Sherleen on the radio. He was not successful.

When Craig finished with his last patient before lunch, he and Jim hurried the four miles to the airport to see what they could find out. Sherleen was already thirty-eight minutes late. But except for a garbled and scratchy transmission from someone saying something about a flight plan, nothing had been heard.

Craig and Jim decided to retrace Sherleen's air route. By about four o'clock they were back where they had started, with nothing new to go on.

Deanna Humes began contacting the Civil Air Patrol. After several calls she reached Don Kent, in charge of the Utah CAP headquartered in Salt Lake City. They had met before, when Don had been helplessly strapped in the back seat of a plane that had crashed at Huntington when the Humes were in charge of that airport. As a result of that experience, Don had felt impelled to finish all his pilot ratings and become personally involved in the CAP, an agency of the U.S. Air Force. Though the CAP is funded and operated by the Air Force, the participants are non-paid volunteers.

Deanna, relieved to talk to a familiar and friendly voice, was assured that Don would do all he could to help. The search would begin at once. As soon as Don could notify them, several planes began searching in assigned grids (one square inch on a World Aeronautical Chart) near the Four Corners area.

5

Her fingernails neatly filed, Sherleen began to get acquainted with her new surroundings. Lush and green, the place spilled over with wildflowers of many colors, quaking aspens, a few tall pines, and oak brush two and three feet deep covering the ground.

A cow wandered by, then some deer. Knowing that watering troughs are placed wherever there are range animals, Sherleen wondered where the troughs were, sure that these animals were passing to or from the water. She hoped she would be able to walk to the trough herself soon. But she'd probably be found before that. The heavy heat of the day was only a minor discomfort amid her more serious problems and painful injuries, yet she began feeling just a little thirsty and dehydrated.

The peculiar chirring of a helicopter sounded overhead. Probably out of Grand Junction, she thought. As the afternoon dragged on, four or five other planes flew over. They too were probably looking for her.

Carefully Sherleen combed through her purse to determine exactly what she had with her. She found an apple and seventeen sticks of gum. A can of soda pop was supposed to be kept in the airplane at all times, but the last person to drink the soda while in flight had not replaced it. With nothing to drink, she decided to save the apple for awhile, but she knew that it was important to chew on something to keep her mouth from swelling up, so she unwrapped a stick of gum and slipped it into her mouth.

Also in her purse she discovered two small miracles: a tiny tube of Mycolog, a medicated ointment, and an Avon chapstick. She decided to do what she could do to dress her wounds. With her nail clippers she cut the top of every wound, squeezing tightly to get out all the pus she could, then put a tiny drop of Mycolog on each one. She also doctored a cold sore that was developing and rubbed some chapstick on her dry lips.

The afternoon wore on, and darkness began settling in over Sherleen's forested niche. She realized the search would have to be abandoned for the night, so she began making plans to sleep. Replacing her first stick of gum with a fresh one, she reasoned that she'd be warmer if she slept by the airplane, where her back would be protected. She began dragging herself toward the plane, wincing at the knifelike pain in the top of her leg. She hauled along a big stick in case she should need to scare off any wild animals.

Once again Sherleen turned to her Heavenly Father in prayer, struggling as she had often done throughout the day to get up on just one knee. She had been taught to pray on her knees, and she thought that perhaps the Lord would be more apt to listen to her if she made every effort to approach Him correctly. With concentrated determination she hoisted herself up to thank Him once again for her life and to beg that His comforting care might be with her through the night. At once a comforting peace settled over her. Deeply moved by this quieting of her fear of being alone, she sat and contemplated in amazement how dependent we are on Him. *He doesn't just protect us from a plane crash*, she thought. *He protects us as we safely drive to work, as the children go safely to and from school every day, as they play, as we . . .*

Overflowing once again with gratitude, Sherleen opened her mouth and sang out into the night:

I know my Father lives and loves me too;
The Spirit whispers this to me
And tells me it is true,
And tells me it is true.

As she closed her eyes, secure in the knowledge that she was being watched and cared for, her thoughts turned again to home and to Jim. She slept only fitfully, as part of her mind tried long into the night to communicate a message to him: *Jim, I'm only fifteen minutes outside of Grand*

13

Junction. Only fifteen minutes out of Grand Junction. Only fifteen minutes . . .

6

Even on a long summer day darkness eventually comes, but to the anxious group gathered at the Price airport it seemed as though the sun was disappearing far too soon. The afternoon had stretched long and tedious, compounding the worry of relatives and friends whose hearts were heavy with concern. Yet darkness had fallen suddenly, forcing them to admit that wherever she was, Sherleen was going to have to spend the night alone.

Reluctantly Jim Jaussi yielded up his hopes for the day and turned to thoughts of the next day. "We have a good chance of finding her tomorrow," he remarked to friends at the airport, "but after that—well, after that, it would take a miracle."

As he drove toward home, he forced himself to set aside his own grief and consider their five children. He couldn't allow himself to yield to the panic arising within him when questions that began with "what if . . ." thrust their way past his hope for tomorrow's search. Yet he didn't want to arouse any false hopes.

As soon as he entered the house and explained that the search that day had been unsuccessful, he told Jan, who, at thirteen, was the oldest child, "Honey, if the impact of the crash has not killed her already, Mom may easily die of injuries or exposure before we can find her. We all want to believe differently, but such a possibility must be faced."

Jan nodded, her eyes brimming with tears. Her father's words were like a nightmare come true. Only a year earlier Jim's sister had died, leaving a family of nine children, including a boy just two years older than Jan.

The sorrow her cousins had felt then reappeared now as her own. How could she bear it? No one knew her as her mother did. They were best friends. They shared shopping trips and long talks. *What will I do without her?* Jan kept asking herself.

Judy, eleven, and Jean, eight, were not told of the extreme seriousness of the situation. Possessing much of their mother's fierce determination, they could only be angry that she would not be coming home due to some circumstance beyond her control. The two youngest children, six-year-old James and three-year-old Jeffrey, found it difficult to believe that Daddy had not been able to find Mommy.

Knowing that the search for Sherleen would be on the evening television news, Jim asked relatives to notify Sherleen's mother, Lola Hoskins, in Georgetown, Idaho. His own mother, Jean Jaussi, had been notified in Laketown, Utah, by her bishop, and she was already on her way to Price.

As she drove, Jean Jaussi recalled the bishop's words, "Sherleen has gone down in her airplane," and her own reaction, "Oh, no, I can't go through all this again." She thought about the nine months since her daughter Diana had died, and how she had gone to stay with the distraught family for a while, trying to be a mother to the children, seeing that they were clean, fed, comforted. Recently their father had remarried, and their lives were being rebuilt. Could she face another tragedy in her family so soon?

In Coalville she stopped to see another son, John, and he insisted that his wife, Sandy, accompany her. They arrived in Price at midnight. Jim and the children were still up, confused and frustrated by Sherleen's absence. Jean at once set about seeing the children to bed. Then she turned to Jim, and mother and son talked long into the night. She

15

was deeply touched by his wisdom and strength, and she agreed with him that the children should be cared for as normally and pleasantly as possible.

"Jan is terribly upset," he told her. "Let her go off and do whatever she wants and needs to do. We won't ask her to take any responsibility right now while she's hurting so much. Judy and Jean are young enough that this is not real to them—let them stay at their friends' homes as long as they want to. Let's help them avoid the confusion around here until Sherleen is found. The boys can just play in the cul-de-sac as usual."

As they talked about Sherleen, Jean could see that Jim was hopeful, but desperate. She went to her room knowing that he would sleep little if at all.

Jim did indeed find sleep nearly impossible as he thought about Sherleen and wondered what was happening to her. Only two possibilities seemed likely: she was either dead, or she was so seriously injured that those injuries could cause her to die soon anyway. He knelt beside his bed—their bed, empty and unfriendly without Sherleen. From deep within his heart he prayed to his Father in heaven. He expressed his sweet pleasure in taking care of Sherleen, and how he had always loved doing things for her and providing for her. Sherleen was always very appreciative, and being able to care for her was one of life's ultimate experiences for Jim.

Now he begged, "Heavenly Father, since I'm no longer able to do these things for her, would you please watch over her for me? Bless her, protect her, keep her warm."

Jim had no doubts whatever about the Lord's ability to do what was necessary for Sherleen, if it were His will. The agonizing part was that Jim did not know what His will was, and he prayed now with renewed determination that he would have the strength to accept whatever it was.

Then more thoughts tumbled into his mind, and he continued praying. Although his first concern was for Sherleen, a very great problem would be the care of their children should she die. The daily needs of the family were something he was always able to depend on Sherleen to handle, as his profession took almost all of his time. Babies come at any hour—night or day—and the constant care of his own children would be difficult, if not impossible, for Jim with a schedule so full and unpredictable.

"Please, *please* bring her back to me," he cried out. "I barely have time to play a little with the kids and to attend to my church responsibilities. How will I *ever* find the time to feed them, bathe them, put them to bed, answer all their needs, and take care of the house? Sherleen does all those things *for* me." The magnitude of the responsibility nearly overwhelmed him, and he felt alone and very, very humble. He recognized his extreme dependence upon the Lord and His power, and he again pleaded for the strength he would need to accept His will.

Exhausted, Jim crawled into the bed. As he lay upon the fresh, clean sheets decorated with apricot and blue flowers, he wondered what Sherleen was covering herself with. The terrible thought that she had no bedding, no food, no water, no comforts was almost too much for him to bear. Oh, if only he could share with her now!

Jim was grateful that he didn't have to wish that he had treated her better, or that he had told her that he loved her. *Sherleen and I have been good to each other*, he thought, *and we've been good for each other.* Jim had loved their eighteen years together. What he wanted more than anything at this moment was the assurance of at least eighteen more.

Wednesday, June 24

1

At 5:30 in the morning Craig and Deanna Humes met once again at the Carbon County airport with one of their student pilots. This time it was Dr. James Jaussi they were joining, and today's planned mission differed dramatically from the graduation flight of only twenty-four hours ago. To the little group preparing to begin their search, it seemed that Sherleen had been missing much longer than that. They were impatient now to be on their way and bring the nightmare to its end.

Jim announced matter-of-factly that he felt Sherleen was just fifteen minutes outside Grand Junction, but he wanted to avoid flying in any area the CAP was searching, as he didn't want them to pull out. Craig had gone over the map the night before and thought perhaps she could have been blown off her course and just missed Blanding, so they decided to do some looking in that area. But first they

18

planned to retrace her flight, hoping to make some kind of new discovery. Since Sherleen's emergency locator transmitter had not gone off indicating a problem, the group was hopeful.

Ted Madsen, a friend and fellow doctor, brought emergency medical equipment along in case it was needed. He had also packed a lunch with plenty of chilled sodas, as he planned to find Sherleen before noon and have a picnic with her.

Deanna flew with other searchers directly to Blanding, while Craig headed toward Grand Junction with Jim, Ted, and a young man named Leland McKay all acting as spotters. Because it was the same time of day and the same type of weather, Craig hoped that flying the same route as Sherleen had taken would help them decide what may have happened.

2

Sherleen could hardly believe the sun was up already. She was sure she had not slept at all. But as she became more awake, she also became more aware of how sore she was. Everything that hadn't hurt yesterday hurt today. She was also very stiff, not only from yesterday's ordeal, but from sleeping on the hard, rocky ground and from working so hard to keep her injured leg in the least painful positions.

The cold hadn't helped. After about two o'clock in the morning she had been so cold she began to fear that she might freeze to death, and shivering from the chill sent excruciating pains through her leg. Even the window coverings hadn't helped much. She had thought about them the night before, happy to remember the existence of any material besides her own clothing that she might use for coverings. It was awkward and painful to crawl back inside the crippled craft, but she had managed to remove one large and two small window coverings. She had also pulled out the cardboard box, the contents of which she had tidied up after the landing yesterday. In it she found a roll of black electrical tape, a welcome sight, and she had used the tape to secure the window shades around her legs to help ward off the chill. But even with those and with the jacket that she had taken with her on her flight, she had still been very cold.

Thank goodness she had run back into the house for her glasses! Her hands were so dirty and her mouth so dry that it would have been very difficult to insert her contacts. She had taken them out the night before and now realized that she had worn her glasses all night. She would have felt terribly helpless now without them. She looked with renewed awareness at the world around her. How blessed she was to have eyes to see the beautiful things the Lord had created. She sang as she had done the night before—not in her heart to herself, but with boldness and gratitude:

The world is so lovely, I'm glad as could be
That I can be here and the lovely things see!
The flowers, the sunshine, the blue sky above,
All make me so happy, my heart fills with love!

Then the love and appreciation she felt for her Heavenly Father prompted her to sing again:

I know my Father lives and loves me too;
The Spirit whispers this to me
And tells me it is true,
And tells me it is true.

Sherleen was happy. She was alive, she still had all of

her faculties, and her body was intact. She had been through a very serious accident yesterday, and the Lord had allowed her to live through it. She was all right, and she knew that she was all right. But it hurt to realize that her family did not have that same knowledge. She had spent much of the night going over in her mind the miracles of the Savior. Especially meaningful to her was the story of Lazarus, of how the Savior had gone to his home after his body had already begun to decay, and yet had raised him from the dead. *I know I can be found,* Sherleen had silently prayed, *if it is Thy will. I know that Thou canst work miracles.* She had prayerfully asked that it might be soon, so that her family would not have to suffer in sorrow and uncertainty. And throughout the night she had consciously continued to try to share her thoughts with Jim and communicate her location to him.

A large ant crawled across Sherleen's leg, and she was suddenly aware of swarms of mosquitoes and flies nearby. The mosquitoes bothered her, but she found herself having a different attitude toward flies than she had ever experienced before. She watched with fascination as they played on her arms. Many things that would normally have frightened or annoyed her seemed different now. Even the thought of snakes and wild animals was not upsetting. She recalled sensing an animal passing close by during the night and thinking to herself, *There goes a deer.* A coyote had even howled earlier. A peaceful feeling enveloped her, and the forest creatures became her friends. More deer had passed by already this morning, and Sherleen was certain that they had come a little closer than the day before.

The plane wreckage was not a pleasant place to be, and Sherleen moved painfully away from it toward the tree where she had sat yesterday, dragging the box and her

21

leg over the rough ground. Once there, she rested, still in shock, slipping in and out of sleep throughout the day. When she built up enough ambition and energy again, she went to work spreading the largest of the window coverings on the ground with the silver side up and placing rocks all around the edges to hold it in place. With the dense forest above her, a spotter would be able to see her signal only if a plane were searching directly overhead, but that was all she could do, except use her small purse mirror as a reflector. She kept it in her hands now, knowing that the search would begin early in the morning before the heat bouncing off the ground created turbulence too dangerous for low flying.

She had heard how difficult searches are. The planes would fly at altitudes only 500 feet above the ground at most, and often lower than that, going slowly up and down an assigned grid only a wingspan apart each time. Listening to the sound of the planes coming now, she could tell what direction they were coming from. She pulled her map out of the box and studied it carefully. From the sounds, she knew that Grand Junction was definitely in the direction she had thought it was. She had not been entirely sure, for after takeoff she had flown at eighty-five miles an hour for fifteen minutes and then had turned completely upside down with the plane, which could have been totally disorienting. Now she was certain her directions were correct.

At midday the sounds of the search planes died away, and the only aircraft she heard were commercial jets flying between Salt Lake City and Denver. She thought about the passengers inside, knowing that a stewardess was offering them something cold to drink. She grimaced at the irony of some of them turning it down. *I'd love to accept a soda pop from her right now*, Sherleen thought. She began to think of those aircraft as "pop jets," resenting their sounds because they only reminded her of her thirst.

Now she could do nothing but wait. The search would not resume till later in the afternoon. She placed her mirror on the silver fabric, in case she dozed off, kept her mouth chewing on the gum, and worked for a while on her open wounds, using the nail clippers and Mycolog, as she had done several times already. She longed for her scriptures—what wonderful company they would be. She owned a small white pocket-size Book of Mormon, which nearly always went from purse to purse wherever Sherleen went, but she had not put it into her purse yesterday.

Sherleen rested her head against a log. As she began to drift off, she thought about her father and Jim's, both of whom were deceased. She wondered if they were aware of her situation now. Half asleep, she found herself sharing her feelings with them, telling them how badly she wanted to go home.

3

The CAP allows outside planes to be involved in a search providing the whereabouts of each aircraft is known to the CAP at all times. Several planes were in the air from Price and surrounding areas, in addition to those officially with the CAP. Those who could not take to the air supplied airplanes for others more available or capable than themselves.

Lynn Dayton, Jim's partner, wanted desperately to be in the air assisting with the search, but since they were the only two obstetricians in the county, his contribution came in maintaining their joint practice. He sent his plane up with pilots approved by the Kepplers, who ran the local airport.

After retracing Sherleen's flight plan, Jim and his group landed in Blanding. Discouraged, they sat down with Deanna Humes for a soft drink and to share their morning's activities. Deanna and her flight companions had checked out several false leads and then contacted the CAP to learn that the search was still concentrated on the area just outside Grand Junction. Jim was glad about that.

The planes were soon in the air again, flying low and slowly in the heavy heat. After flying more grids south of Blanding and then north toward Grand Junction, the Cherokee piloted by Craig Humes developed battery problems. He and Deanna sent the others home while they stayed in Grand Junction searching for a mechanic.

Parting was difficult. Jim's words of the night before kept ringing in his friend's ears. "We have a good chance of finding her tomorrow, but after that it would take a miracle," he had said. Now the search on that day of the "good chance" had to be abandoned, leaving only the time for miracles.

As Craig saw Jim head off toward Price without Sherleen, he agonized over whether he had done the right thing in sending Sherleen alone the day before. Had she gone by herself too soon? Had he missed something in her training? Was he responsible for the fact that she was missing now? He had tried to cover everything—had even had her fly with a hood on and land on a dirt road as though the engine had gone out. But he still couldn't help wondering if he was somehow responsible for what had happened.

4

Sherleen was awakened by the rumbling of an engine. It wasn't a plane—more like a tractor. The noise grew louder and more distinguishable, until she could finally recognize it: a Caterpillar! *What's a Caterpillar doing in a forest?* Her thoughts were interrupted by another familiar sound—electric saws, not too far away. Excited, she began to yell, "Help, help, over here—help!" But when her voice was hoarse and her throat sore, she had to laugh at herself to think that anyone might actually hear her over the sound of a motor.

By late afternoon she could hear the drone of search planes again, and she waited patiently for them to see her. She knew that she must be found by eight-thirty, because by dusk the planes would have to return to the airport. If the searchers had to fly any distance home that night, such as to Price, an hour away, they would have to quit even earlier. But these planes now were getting so close! They were covering an area just west of where she sat, and as she checked her watch, she could see that it took them five minutes to go from one end of the grid to the other. Her excitement grew each time they were due to return, for they were gradually drawing nearer. Only a few more moments and they would be flying directly overhead!

But suddenly they didn't return on time, and Sherleen sagged in disappointment. Once again the search had been called off because of darkness. Her disappointment didn't last long, however, as she reasoned that they would start tomorrow where they had left off and cross right above her. "They'll finish that grid," she told herself, "and they'll find me, first thing in the morning."

Her excitement about being found was not the only special thing to end her second day in the woods. She had promised herself that she would not touch the apple until Wednesday night, and Wednesday night had now arrived. Before she went to bed, she would have some of it. Dragging her box, she crawled as quickly as she could to the side of the plane where she had slept the night before. She wrapped and taped the window coverings around her legs, then slowly and deliberately bit into the cherished fruit. It tasted more wonderful than she had imagined. She allowed herself to eat half of it, looking off into the shadows as she chewed, alone with her feast.

5

Lola Hoskins, Sherleen's mother, arrived in Price shortly after noon on Wednesday. Jean Jaussi greeted her and together they shared their despair and deep emotions. There were so many questions and so few answers. *Where is she? What are her chances? What will Jim do? What kind of a life will the family have without Sherleen? What are we going to do without her?*

Lola worried that Sherleen would be hungry and cold. She was also concerned that Sherleen's face not be disfigured, and she told Jean that she had been praying for that since learning of Sherleen's disappearance. Jean, who shared her son's growing fears that Sherleen was dead, was concerned for those who remained behind.

The two women didn't face the usual care of a home and family. There was no need to prepare food. A fast had been called by the Jaussis' bishop beginning Tuesday night and was scheduled to continue through this evening. Food for future days would not be a problem, for the Relief Society president had lined up volunteers to provide meals for each of the next several days. Jean insisted, "That's really not necessary. No one here is eating. And there may be a time soon when we need it more than we do now." But the food came. And not just from the Relief Society, but from many sources. People brought whatever they thought could be used, and along with each morsel came their love, their hopes, and their support.

What the two women did keep busy with was answering the telephone and greeting concerned people at the door, as many caring people reached out, hoping to hear good news.

Although the day had been an exhausting one, members of the Jaussi family prepared to attend the prayer meeting at seven o'clock at the church to close the ward fast. Facing more people and more questions was difficult, but seeing the strength and faith of so many who were united in their concern for Sherleen was also comforting.

No one spoke as the congregation filed into the meetinghouse, and by the appointed hour, the room was filled. The only children in attendance were the younger Jaussis, but most of the adults of the ward appeared to be present. The Young Women were all there to show their love and support for Sherleen, their leader. Jan slipped into the rear of the chapel with her friends as the meeting began.

It had been a long, very hot day, and ward members who had craved a drink of water throughout the fast found themselves reminded of how thirsty Sherleen must be.

Bishop Crookston conducted the short service. He called the meeting to order and asked Joe Goodrich, one of the Jaussis' home teachers, to offer a prayer to conclude the fast. Together members of the ward family knelt and offered up their united petitions.

Lynn Lemon, the elders quorum president, and his wife, Susan, told the Jaussi family after the prayer that they felt certain Sherleen was still alive. Though they were concerned for her well-being, they didn't feel the panic and despair they were sure they would have felt if she were dead. In fact, they were so sure that she was not dead that they prayed fervently for the Lord's help in understanding the feelings they were experiencing lest they fill others with false hopes. The more they prayed about it, the

27

stronger their convictions grew that Sherleen was going to be all right. Though he didn't mention it at the time, Lynn had seen Sherleen leaning against a tree as he prayed about her, and Susan had seen her in a dream. Jean Jaussi felt a moment of hope. *Maybe they do know*, she thought. *Maybe the Spirit has gotten through to them.* She felt a calmness that she hadn't experienced for two days. Then she went home and remembered how hot the day had been, and what a small plane Sherleen had been flying, and . . .

6

After the Cherokee was ready to go again, Craig and Deanna headed home to Price. Neither spoke as they flew over oil wells, a river, and deep canyons. So many things that were normally beautiful now appeared threatening as they wondered if this place or that might have claimed their friend. Accepting what seemed to be the inevitable would be difficult.

As they drove home from the airport in their van, Craig broke the stillness. "Why did this happen? Why? She was so good, and she did nothing but good on the earth."

"Perhaps Sherleen had nothing more to learn and do here. Perhaps she has a new mission elsewhere." Deanna hoped Craig would understand what she was saying. These thoughts were somewhat foreign, even to her, and she was suddenly very sorry for that. Craig was not a member of the Church, and since their marriage she had slipped further and further away from a life-style and concepts that had once been so important to her. The comforting feeling that Jim radiated came from an inner peace and faith that was so very much a part of him, and Deanna wanted the same kind of faith in her own life again.

Her thoughts were interrupted as Craig agonized

again over the question that continued to haunt him. "Why did it have to be in an airplane?"

Deanna thought for a long time before she answered. "Maybe it was to get *our* attention, Craig. Is there any other way He could reach *us*? Who else will be more affected than we will, if she's been killed in an airplane?"

Thursday, June 25

1

Don Kent continued to direct the Civil Air Patrol search from his Salt Lake office, coordinating the efforts of volunteers from three states—Utah, Colorado, and Arizona. This morning, he telephoned the grid map to Craig and Jim at the Price airport at 5:30 A.M.

The Cherokee, owned by the Jaussis and the Madsens, was again piloted by Craig Humes. Accompanying him today were Deanna as well as Jim Jaussi and Ted Madsen. They headed toward Vernal to fly their assigned grids along with a CAP plane piloted by a man named Ott Webb. Deanna felt somewhat rested, having taken a sleeping pill the night before—she knew she could not have slept otherwise. But she worried now about Craig, who had not dared take any substance that might hinder his ability to pilot the plane.

Ted Madsen was his usual positive self, full of plans

and determined that this was the day they would find Sherleen. Jim was less enthusiastic. Sherleen's situation, he knew, had become more serious with each passing hour. His medical training forced him to confront facts that haunted him. Sherleen had been down for nearly forty-eight hours. If she had somehow survived death on impact, she was now beginning her third day without water. Jim had been forcing himself to abstain from drinking in order to know better what might be happening to Sherleen. Flying all day long inside the small Cherokee in the hot summer weather was resulting in intense dehydration. He had also eaten very little since Tuesday. He not only had no *desire* for food, but he also couldn't help feeling a twinge of guilt with each bite he took, thinking of how hungry Sherleen must be. He realized, however, that he had to eat enough to keep his strength up. If he were to become sick, he would be useless in the search.

After several hours in the air, the spotters found that they could now see and identify objects on the ground quite accurately. Yesterday Jim had been certain he had spotted Sherleen standing beside her airplane. His hopes turned to disappointment when what he had seen turned out to be nothing more than the stump of a telephone pole beside a silver storage tank with ladders up each side. As they methodically covered the area of each grid, the searchers spotted people rafting on the Green River, horses swishing their tails, and many old wrecked automobiles. They were amazed at the tons of trash strewn about the wilderness—broken glass that reflected the sunlight, parts of destroyed vehicles, and they wondered how it had all gotten there.

Spotting for ten or twelve hours a day while cramped in a small plane is extremely taxing to the body, making one's neck, head, and back very sore. The searchers longed

31

to close their eyes for just a few moments, but they didn't dare, knowing that they might miss the spot Sherleen was in and never see it again.

Ott Webb's attitude, as the planes flew the grids together, provided a lot of comfort and reassurance to the foursome in the Cherokee. His dedication in covering the outlined territory as carefully as possible gave them great hope, especially as they thought of how many CAP pilots were participating in the search. Ott hated to leave a grid. Before he finished searching an area and crossed it off, he wanted to be absolutely sure Sherleen was not in it. Making that final decision to leave an area was a matter of utmost concern to him. After this search came to an end, he planned to retire. He had searched with the CAP for forty years and had never found a survivor—many crashes, but never a survivor. He desperately wanted this last experience to be a successful one.

2

Sherleen had spent a most uncomfortable night. In addition to the bruises and injuries from the crash, she had had excruciating cramps and pains all night long as a result of gobbling up half of the apple before going to sleep. *I'll never do that again*, she vowed. *It was delicious, but certainly not worth all the suffering it caused!* In the future, when she allowed herself some of the apple, she would only suck each bite and then spit out the pulp. She'd have to get her chewing needs filled with gum. As the sun gradually warmed her, she forced herself to keep chewing what remained of last night's allotted stick until eight o'clock. Then she'd allow herself a new one. She looked forward to refreshing the taste in her mouth.

Despite her discomfort, Sherleen felt rejuvenated, hopeful. "Today will be the day!" she declared to the forest around her. If there were nothing for her to look forward to, she could literally have slept her life away, but listening for the search planes to come closer and closer kept her alive and alert.

As on the previous two mornings after the sun had awakened and warmed her, she moved to her spot by the tree. When it became unbearably hot as the day wore on, she dragged herself on her one good hip farther and farther into the trees to cool off a bit, scooting her box of belongings with her, gingerly holding her sore finger free as she clawed her way along in the dirt and brush.

Sitting by the tree this morning, she eagerly awaited the search planes. But they had *not* resumed their path directly over her. They were farther away! Sherleen was stunned. She was so sure she'd be found this morning. For the first time since the crash two days ago, she gave way to despair and began sobbing uncontrollably, her cries of disappointment, loneliness, and fatigue echoing in the wilderness.

Finally, feeling washed and relieved, she began to relax, and the sobbing ceased. She forced her thoughts away from the disappointment and turned once again to the beauty around her and the glories of the creation. Suddenly her eyes met with those of a magnificent buck. Standing next to him was another, smaller buck. They eyed the intruder with great curiosity. The smaller of the two animals was a two-point buck; both deer were all the more beautiful because of the rich velvet that still adorned their antlers. Sherleen watched the deer continue on in majesty, marveling at how gorgeous they were. She found herself singing again the two songs she had come to love more than ever before. Then she sang a third beloved song, "I Am a Child of God."

The last song, a family favorite, made her think of her own children at home. It had been so wonderful to have them all with her last night. She had known it was only a dream even as it was happening, but it was wonderful anyway. The children had found her and then had gone for a walk. Suddenly, they came running back to her with jubilation in their voices and told her of a farmhouse they had found. Eager to share it with her, they wanted to carry her down to see it. All the while Sherleen kept telling herself not to be disappointed when she awakened and they were gone.

Later in another dream, Jan washed and put up Sherleen's hair for her. What a pleasure it was to enjoy that for a few moments.

Sherleen missed her children so much right now that she thought her heart would burst. She remembered a little notebook in her purse. Quickly pulling it and her pen out, she leaned her head against a log and began to write to the family who waited at home for her. First came a note to her eldest daughter, a blossoming young woman not quite thirteen, who, at five feet, seven inches, was already several inches taller than her mother.

Jan,

How I love you! I want you to be a success in all that you do. Each day work on a worthy goal—reading, piano, or something else good that you want to accomplish.

Listen to your good father. He is only interested in you and wants the best for you in life. He is a very good father and will lead you in the right way if you will listen.

I love you with all my heart.

Mother

When Sherleen had finished writing to her firstborn, she turned the page over and added a promise, to be fulfilled if indeed she should be found alive: "Jan, I give you three shopping trips without once saying, 'Let's hurry!'"

34

Judy's letter came next, and as the words began to fill the little page, Sherleen pictured her busy eleven-year-old, always bustling from one activity to another. With her brown eyes and hair, Judy is the darkest of the Jaussi children.

Judy,

How I love my faithful helper. You are always so loyal and good to me. I appreciate all your endless help. It makes my life much easier. You are extremely dependable. This is a great attribute and will take you far.

Judy, follow the advice of Daddy. He sincerely loves you and wants you to be successful in life.

Know of my love for you.

Mother

And on the back, Sherleen added: "Judy, how about a Slurpee a week? Think even I will grow to like them!"

Sherleen addressed the next note to her quiet little eight-year-old Jean. A tiny child, with light brown hair like Jan and James, Jean had a row of freckles across the bridge of her nose to match her mother's.

Jean,

My little sweet undemanding Jean. You are such a joy to be around and bring such peace to those around you. What a quieting spirit you add to our family.

I love you so very much. I love you to put your little hand in mine when you want to walk somewhere in the house with me. I'm glad you want me to kiss you goodnight.

You are a special love to me.

Mother

Jean's promise read: "Jean, I want to watch you fix your hair a special way each day!"

35

James, his father's namesake and eager helper, was the older of the two boys. At age six, he was built like a linebacker and was in constant motion. Sherleen ached for the touch of his fat little hand, which was frequently reaching for hers.

James,

Oh, what would I do without those big hugs and kisses you so freely give to me.

You are a very smart young man. It is fun to see you read, do your math, and learn so quickly.

It is special to have a healthy big boy around the house. You make each day so special.

You say such beautiful prayers each night. I love to listen to them.

I love you very much.

Mother

Remembering how rushed the evenings had all too often been, Sherleen added on the back: "James, I want to read you a story each night."

The mother smiled as she thought of Jeffrey, at three the baby of the family. They had all enjoyed letting him grow up slowly, and Sherleen relished his company. He was always eager to see what was going on in the kitchen, and it suddenly seemed silly that she had ever been annoyed at his sitting on the counter next to her. A little bit of mess or even a few germs in the food could not possibly be that important! She mentioned that in her note to the little brown-eyed boy:

Jeffrey,

My second Jan. What a joy you are to me. I'm glad you like to be around me, to take my hand as we go down to do the wash, and to follow me around the house.

36

I love your lively little body. It is busy and involved but so special to me.

Cooking wouldn't be fun without you on the cabinet to help me.

I love you, my special little blond.

Mother

The back of his letter invited Jeffrey to join in the story time with her and James.

Sherleen and Jim had been blessed with five happy, healthy children, each one a beautiful part of the joy in their lives. But as Sherleen mused on the blessings the children had brought into their lives, she began to feel guilty. Jim wanted to add a sixth child to their family, but she had not wanted to have any more babies. One of the conditions upon which she agreed to move from Salt Lake City to Price was that she not hear any more about having another child. Jim had kept his promise. Now suddenly Sherleen found herself making one of her own. If she could be rescued alive, she vowed, she would have that sixth baby with Jim.

As she thought of her loving, devoted husband and of his wise and kindly ways, she shared her thoughts with him on paper also. Far into the day she wrote, telling him of the things that were in her heart and of her life the past several hours:

Dear Jim,

May I first tell you how much I love you. You not only make me happy, but make life worth living. You have always been so good to me, whether I have deserved it or not.

I hope with all my heart you won't give up until you find me, so I can have a chance to love you, enjoy you, and grow old with you.

This has been the worst experience I have ever had,

37

and I know, because of how you love me, that this has been hard for you too. I only wish it could never have happened. I've talked to you day and night hoping I could some way reach you, and you would know where to look for me.

I have been thirsty, hungry, cold, and lonely, but not frightened. Only frightened that I would not be found—and that is a terribly frightening feeling.

I have prayed so hard to my Father in heaven many times. I know He loves me, and I just can't believe He would let me live through the crash only to let me die from thirst and hunger. I know He is all powerful and can do all things. I know He will not forget me at this time.

The emergency transmitter on the plane never worked—oh, how disappointing. The flashlight batteries were gone too.

She wrote of her feelings the morning of her flight and of the actual accident. She mentioned, "Oh, well, we all make mistakes. Some are fatal, some are not. Mine won't be if I can just be found."

She told Jim what she had learned:

Maybe I've learned a little patience. This has been very hard for me to sit here with nothing to do. The time drags on—except when I hear planes searching and the time goes too fast and it gets later in the day and soon they have to return home.

Then the long endless night comes. I dream of being in a clean bed next to you—warm and being snuggled, knowing of your love for me. I pray I will have that marvelous experience again.

I dreamed last night that the children were with me. Only a short distance from here was a ranch and the children had found it—then to awaken and be so alone again!

I dream of big tall glasses of ice water, Sprite, and

Catch. I think I will forever eat anything and all I want from now on. Oh, I hope I don't have to starve to death. I don't care that you have a little pudgy tummy.

I'm so dirty and such a mess. I don't even have a comb. Last night I dreamed Jan was washing and curling my hair.

One grows to love and appreciate the little things after an experience such as this. Oh, I hope I am found. (The planes keep going all around me but never right over me— why?) Jim, with all my heart I pray and beg you won't stop looking until I'm found.

Sherleen talked about their life in Price, about her feelings toward flying, about many other things. Then:

If I'm not found before I'm gone, Jim—please choose someone very carefully who will be good to our children. I want them to be good and taught correct principles, but I also want them to be happy. I can hardly bear the thought that maybe I won't see you or them again. The idea makes me ache and hurt all over. I want to go home so badly. I haven't given up yet. I can go many more days without food and water. (But I'd love a beautiful big drink of something you made to surprise me—a fresh lime, maybe?)

When I first got out of the plane, my right shoulder was out of place, but after a while I was able to move it just right, and it went back in. It hasn't hurt, either. My left leg is extremely painful if I try to stand on it or move it the wrong way. I have to slide on my bottom everywhere I go. It takes a long time, but then, where do I have to go anyway? I think the big muscle in my left leg on the inside was torn some way, because the leg doesn't seem to be broken. Oh, just to have my Jim look at it and tell what is wrong!

I would guess Grandma Jaussi is in Price with the little people. I know she will be good to them.

Thursday

Many planes—well, about six—have gone all around me so I could really see them, but not one has flown right over where I am. I hope that will be you, Jim, so you will instantly know I'm okay! I truly do love you!

Remember, dear, to send Wayne $100.00 a month. It goes to Karolyn. Sovereigns' address is in the top right hand desk drawer in the little middle sections. It is still on the deposit slip Sandeye wrote the original address on. The bills for the piano and Culligan water are in the big middle drawer at the back in the middle. They are both in a white envelope with black writing on it.

Oh, for a bath full of Jean Naté bath crystals! Here it is one o'clock and I just put my contacts in. Thank goodness I ran up quickly (as I am always doing) and got my glasses. So I have worn them really a lot. I'm wearing my contacts just enough to keep up my wearing time. I'm almost too dirty to put them in.

Another plane just went by. They are always to the south of me. Why won't one fly so they can see me?

It is quite cloudy. Please don't rain, because they will stop looking and then I will be all wet. My leg hurts too much to fold up to crawl into the plane. Please go away, clouds. It is after one. The day will soon be gone and again I'm still here. The nights are so horrible. I wish I had my scriptures to read.

I keep looking at the time and wondering what my (our) children are doing. I really miss them. I know you are searching for me. Please don't stop!!!!

Honey, keep money in my checking account in Salt Lake so your insurance will be paid. (I love you.)

Sherleen rested. She didn't sign off to Jim; she might write more later. She had spent a great part of the day penning her thoughts to her loved ones, stopping to rest her arm or wipe away some tears. She felt drained, having opened up and poured out her heart. With the sound of a "pop jet" passing overhead, her thoughts reached out to the home on Apple Circle, and she tried to imagine what her children were doing.

3

Judy stayed home all day on Thursday. Up until now, her overt reaction to the whole trauma had been quick questions as she darted in and out past her Grandmother Jaussi.

"Have they found Mother yet?" And when her grandmother would reply that they had not heard from her father yet that day, she'd ask, "Well, when are they going to find her?" Then she would slip back into the routine of life, the nervous energy she had inherited from her mother keeping her going.

Today she was breaking under the strain, beginning to suspect that she might not see her mother again. They had had so many plans, and she clung to them now in desperation as they seemed to be crumbling before her. "My mother promised she'd teach me how to sew," she cried out. "If we can't find her, Grandmother, *you* have to teach me how to sew."

"Don't worry, honey. If we don't find your mother, I'll help you learn to sew. I promise."

Then Judy cried, and not knowing what to do with herself, she announced, "My mother promised she'd take me to the Go-carts." Aching for the child in her frustration, her grandmother took Judy to the Go-carts and let her ride around and around the track.

After Judy and her grandmother returned home, Jan hurried through the house with some friends on the way to get a change of clothes from her bedroom. She had not been a part of the household since Wednesday morning, when the crying, the hugging, the visitors, and the questions had been more than she could handle. She had spoken no more than ten words each day to her grandmother. Jean knew how difficult it was for Jan to see her there in her mother's place. Jan had seen the same thing happen in her cousins' family, and it was hard for her to cope with now that it was happening in her own. Jean recognized and understood her granddaughter's reaction, yet she knew that the responsibilities she was accepting had to be taken by someone. Somebody had to be in the kitchen, and say, "We will have this to eat at this meal" and "We will have that to eat at that meal"; "We will put this in the deep freeze," "We will clean up the dishes now," "We will dust," "We will vacuum." That somebody was Jean, and without her, the children's father would not have been able to devote himself to the search as he needed to. Still, to Jan it remained a nightmare that she wished desperately would end. She resented the reminder her grandmother's presence represented.

Jean was still spending a lot of time on the telephone and talking to people who came to the door with questions, hope, or gifts of food. Sharon Madsen came on Thursday afternoon to share a bit of encouraging information. Until now, the Tomahawk's ELT had been silent. But today Ted had called his wife to say the CAP had been picking up a signal, and they were very hopeful it might be Sherleen's.

As Sharon was leaving, a Pizza Hut delivery truck arrived with four huge pizzas and the sincere hopes and wishes of the owners of the local establishment.

Jean found that she was continually overwhelmed at the kindnesses that were shown to them. Earlier that afternoon, a telegram had arrived from Bishop James Mason and the Salt Lake City ward of which the Jaussis had been members:

"Ensign 6 Ward concerned and anxious about Sherleen. Let us know when to use resources here for ground and air search. We have a capable stand-by group. Our prayers are with you."

People who had never even met Sherleen or anyone else in the Jaussi family reached out in love. Many concerned friends and members of the community worried about disturbing the Jaussi household with calls and questions, so they telephoned the airport to ask what news there might be. Ardith Keppler wanted to keep the airport telephone line free, so gradually a system had evolved whereby she would speak with Margaret Dayton (Jim's partner's wife) about four times a day, and Margaret in turn would notify an ever-expanding network of individuals who would spread the word to others. Mary Louise Ghirardelli, executive secretary, and her boss, John Harris, Castleview Hospital's administrator, were two people who were anxious to help and were kept regularly informed. Hospital personnel knew they could always pass by Mary's desk for the latest word. Margaret also passed the word to several persons from different wards who then carried the message to other anxious ears.

For two days Margaret had received several calls every hour asking, "What can I do? How can I help?" On Thursday when Margaret asked Ardith what people on the ground could do to assist, Ardith mentioned that it would be good to have some food waiting at the airport for the pilots and spotters, so they could grab something quickly before they returned to the air. Margaret quickly made calls to two key people, asking that sandwiches and cookies be brought to her house in two hours. In less than that time, Margaret's four-wheel drive vehicle literally overflowed with boxes and ice chests—roast beef sandwiches, fried chicken, fruits and vegetables, cartons of milk and punch, candy bars, and six homemade cakes, still warm from the oven. By afternoon the word had spread even more, and food continued to pour in from sources that even Margaret knew nothing about. Mary Louise called from the hospital and said, "We understand you are organizing food to take out to the searchers, and the hospital would like to help. Would you prefer boxed lunches or buffet style?"

4

The Cherokee flew persistently up and down the charted grids while inside the cabin Jim Jaussi sat bathed in sweat, his mouth thick with thirst. The temperature in the cabin had to be at least one hundred degrees. "It's probably no worse than what Sherleen is going through," he mused. "If she's alive—but how can she possibly be alive?" he asked himself. "It's more than I dare hope for." His thoughts tumbled one on top of the other, as he gazed steadily out at the earth skimming by beneath him. He watched carefully for every sign, every glimmer, every object that might possibly be the downed Tomahawk.

Alert though he was to the terrain below him, still his mind raced with the unanswered question—"Have I allowed Sherleen to throw her life away?" They had been so confident about their decision to become pilots. He'd heard the comments of several who criticized that decision—"How can a man allow a woman with a good life and five little children to get into an airplane and throw her life away?"

He had decided to have a memorial service to honor Sherleen. He wanted to show his love and respect for her, to tell people that the decision for her to take flying lessons had not been made carelessly or on a whim, that Sherleen was a strong and capable woman. He wanted all the world to know that he had cherished her, that they had been good to each other, that she had been a devoted mother and organized housekeeper. Even while he mulled them over in his head, he knew that such things still could not come close to conveying what he felt for Sherleen—yet he knew he wanted to try.

"What do you think of that idea, Jim?" Ted's voice interrupted Jim's musings. "I was saying how just about everyone in Price has four-wheel-drive vehicles, and they all go into the hills with them on weekends. Let's just have them all go over and drive the mountains near Grand Junction."

Jim was by nature a more cautious individual than Ted, and the idea of a lot of untrained people searching through such rough terrain struck him as a rather frightening responsibility. Ted could see how leery he was of the proposal and decided he'd said enough. "You just give the word, Jim, and we'll get it rolling."

Ted's comment represented more than a passing thought, however. Several people at home, eager to be involved, wanted to put together a ground search. The idea had been evolving in the minds of Ted Madsen and Lynn Lemon for a day or two, and even now many waited in Price for word on such a project.

The Cherokee completed grids 4, 5, 6, 32, and 33 before giving up for the day, and the four searchers headed home exhausted and in low spirits. They all agreed when Craig said he was too worn out mentally and physically to fly as many hours tomorrow as they had been doing up to now. Instead they made plans to go to Grand Junction and listen to the tapes of Sherleen's conversations with the tower the morning of her flight, talk to people at the control tower and others who might have spoken to her at the airport, and see if they could come up with any new ideas.

5

As they had each night, neighbors surrounded Jim when he drove into the cul-de-sac, eager for some word of hope. Tonight young James pushed through the crowd and demanded, "Did you find my mommy yet?" Jim caressed him on the head and answered sadly, "No, son, I didn't."

"You can't find my mommy!" James screamed accusingly, and he ran into the house, slamming the door behind him. Upstairs in his room, he continued angrily, "I want my mommy! I'm so sick of this! I just want my mommy!"

His grandmother tried to comfort him. "James, we're doing everything we can to find your mother."

But James was beyond comfort as he sat on his bed and shrieked out in pain, "I'm not doing one more thing until my mother is found. So don't *anyone* tell me to do one more thing!"

James's cries, clearly audible to his father as well as the neighbors gathered in the street outside, pierced Jim's heart and created a pain of their own. He wanted desperately to console his son, to tell him that his mother would be all right. But he didn't know that himself. What would happen when the wreckage of the plane was finally found? How would he face everyone, especially his children, with the news that Sherleen was dead? How would they react? Could they accept it after so many days of faith and hope?

The children remained adamant that their mother was *not* dead. They refused to listen to any suggestion otherwise. Jim was beginning to fear that they were living a fantasy, protecting themselves from reality by living in a bubble of unrealistic imagination. To him, the realities were cold and vivid. Most victims of small-plane crashes are killed almost instantly. If Sherleen had miraculously managed to survive the impact, she must have been very seriously injured; otherwise she would have found her way to some sort of help, or at least been able to signal the searchers.

The thought of Sherleen lying suffering in the wreckage in temperatures that soared beyond one hundred degrees every day was just too much for Jim to bear. He had to believe that his wife had died immediately on impact. The suffering she would otherwise be enduring was something he could not force himself to contemplate.

Two of the friends who gathered to learn what news Jim had were their next-door neighbors, Brent and Leila Johnson. Brent was the president of the Young Men in the ward and worked closely with Sherleen, his counterpart with the Young Women. Just the previous weekend Sherleen and both Brent and Leila had participated with the young people of the ward in a three-day campout. The Johnsons could not help but recall that experience with a certain sadness now.

Jim exhausted his supply of news about the search, bid his neighbors goodnight, and entered his home to repeat the same news to his mother. Then, as he started up the stairs, he added, "Mother, if she *is* alive, her kidneys will have stopped functioning today."

"Oh, Jim, how can you be so sure?" Jean Jaussi cried out.

Many people go three or more days without food and water during an unusually long fasting period—he himself knew of several. But, he explained, a self-imposed fast in a person's normal setting, for spiritual reasons, differs vastly from being subject to the unbending elements of nature. A person fasting at home receives some degree of replenishment of lost body fluids from taking a bath and brushing his teeth. Even the protection afforded the body by coverings at night stands in marked contrast to the dry-

47

ing influence of hot days and cold nights. His medical training and experience had taught Jim that only a miracle could prevent the shutting down of renal functions from exposure.

Jean nodded, unable to answer her son. She too had come to the same sorrowful conclusion. While they discussed their tragic reasoning, little Jean Jaussi, her grandmother's namesake, stood unseen behind a door. She had been listening carefully and understood what they were saying. But she didn't believe a single word.

Jim prepared for bed, then dropped to his knees, as he had done so many times already, and pleaded with his Father in heaven to know where Sherleen was. As he settled into bed, he felt more strongly than ever that she was just fifteen minutes outside of Grand Junction. He was glad the searchers had decided to go there tomorrow.

In the Madsen home a meeting, somewhat organized and yet with the spontaneity that results from frustration and eagerness, was taking place. Many suggestions were made for the next course of action. Some people wanted to head for the hills that night so that they could be doing something concrete by daybreak. Others were more cautious, preferring to map out a carefully conceived direction. Those who were experienced in such situations were decidedly pessimistic; they warned of the poor chance of finding Sherleen that a group of untrained searchers would have in unfamiliar territory when they didn't even know which of all the areas they should be looking in. A man from the Search and Rescue Unit had been invited to address the group, and he commented, "A search of this type would be ridiculous! We *never* look from the ground until we spot the victim from the air, and even then it's difficult to find him!"

Ridiculous though a ground search seemed, many persisted in their determination to try. A difficult decision

was made. Because the professionals were so strongly op-
posed to a ground search for fear of needlessly endanger-
ing even more lives, Ted and Lynn decided that they could
not take the responsibility of inviting the community at
large to participate, even though many were willing to do
so. They concluded it would be best to simply make it an
elders quorum function, a group of priesthood holders
united in thought and purpose. After the meeting broke
up at about ten o'clock, Susan Lemon and Sharon Madsen
began calling the men in the ward. Their message: "Be
ready to go, and wait for the final decision tomorrow
afternoon."

6

Sherleen heard her stomach growl, and the sound of
it startled her. She wasn't really very hungry. Oh, it would
taste good to eat something, but she didn't feel hungry
enough to warrant the insistent growls that emanated
from her stomach. Though she felt little hunger, she was
certainly thirsty! She continued to chew her gum, and oc-
casionally she held a small bite of apple in her mouth and
sucked on it. Once she pulled on a little grasslike weed
with a fuzzy end and sucked the tiny bit of white moisture
out of the stem. It was surprisingly refreshing. She
chomped on the green part for a while, then spit it out.

Each day Sherleen seemed to feel stronger and more
alert than the day before. Her injuries continued to bother
her and hamper her mobility, but her biggest discomfort
involved the heat and her thirst. The day had been mercilessly hot, but evening brought a slight, refreshing
breeze. Sherleen remembered a recent conversation she'd
had with Jim about BoJo, their combination St. Bernard-
black Labrador, who was sitting with her mouth open and
her tongue hanging out.

"Why does she stick her tongue out like that?" she'd asked.

"That's her air conditioning system," Jim answered. "When she puts her tongue out, the air sweeps across it and cools her entire body."

Sherleen thought it was worth a try. As the evening breeze picked up, she sat with her tongue out, collecting it. *Marvelous*, she told herself, *what you can learn about comfort and survival from a dog!*

It was time to settle down for the night once again. Sherleen asked herself why she should continue to sleep beside the plane wreckage. The terrain was so uncomfortable there, and with all the woods to choose from, there *must* be a better place! She wondered why she had already slept there twice, and realized that in her weaker condition, she must have felt comfort and security in being near the plane. But she had much more confidence and imagination now, and as she thought about the various little areas where she spent different times of the day, she remembered her favorite, a place among some trees where she had crawled to rest as the sun moved around.

She scooted along to the little grove with her box and positioned herself atop the leaves. Earlier she had wondered if this had been a deer's bed, with its generous carpet of soft leaves. Her suspicions appeared to be correct when a doe snorted indignantly at her as she occupied it. She found that she could adjust the leaves under her hip and achieve quite a comfortable position. Ready for the night, she sat in her new bed and gazed off into the darkened trees.

The forest at night reminded her of the youth campout she and her neighbor Leila Johnson had participated in only a week before. She chuckled aloud as she remembered how the two of them had thought they were suffering out in the wilderness. They had slept in nice warm sleeping bags inside a cozy tent. They'd eaten lots of wonderful food and had even taken jars of water to bed with them in case they got thirsty during the night. A little canvas-covered "outhouse" had been constructed for the occasion, and Sherleen thought longingly about the delightfully soft roll of toilet paper that had hung from the limb of a tree. Perhaps the height of their discomfort had been the annoying presence of a few flies inside the tent. "Boy, Leila, we really had it rough, didn't we?" Sherleen laughed aloud and shook her head.

She fell asleep and had the most restful slumber she had enjoyed in three days, despite the fact that the night was wild with thunder. As she slept and dreamed, Bishop Crookston visited and brought her a tall glass of ice water.

Friday, June 26

1

Sherleen awakened Friday morning before sunrise. She had had a comfortable night, and she began scooting her way back toward the plane with revitalized enthusiasm and hope. On her way she saw something that took her totally by surprise—something she had not seen before because she had never been in that particular place at that time of the day. From that vantage point, looking west for the first time, she could see that the sun was already shining in an area about one hundred and twenty-five yards away. Her heart pounded as she considered the implications. *There's a clearing out there! There has to be, because the sun's not up where I am yet. I've got to get to that clearing! If I hurry and get my things together, I can be out there before they start to search!*

She had never felt such excitement in her life as she

gathered together into the box everything she might need as she sat and waited for them to pick her up. Excited though she was, she was still mercilessly thirsty, and she rummaged through the broken cockpit for some cardboard cylinders she had seen there. Recalling the thunder last night, she had decided to try to catch a drink if it rained. She also loaded into the box her purse and a flag that she had fashioned out of a window covering and a stick.

Then she began the tortuous trip out to the clearing. She'd slide gingerly on her bottom, stop and drag the box up next to her, slide, pull, slide, pull, slide, pull . . . *Rough terrain, but can't stop and worry about that now. I've got to get out to that clearing before they do.* She switched places with the box, and that seemed to work better. Pushing the box, then pulling herself up next to it—push, pull up, push, pull up. Gradually she pulled herself out of the tree cover and arrived at the clearing. It had taken forty-five minutes!

The clearing was about twice the size of a football field, bordered on the side farthest from Sherleen by a wire fence. She could barely see the fence, however, because the sagebrush was very tall—so tall that when she noticed a deer moving by, all she could see were its ears. But the sight that caught and held her eye was a rainbow—a magnificent rainbow stretching from one end of the clearing to the other. Rainbows had always been a lucky sign for Sherleen, and as this one soared in the sky before her, she exulted, "This is going to be my rainbow day. I'm going to be found today!"

She was very tired from her trip out of the trees, but she was alive, she had found new hope for being rescued, and she had beaten the search planes to the clearing. Grateful for all of those things and much more, she once again sang her three favorite songs and waited for the searchers to come. Her lonely voice held more conviction than ever as she began, "I know my Father lives and loves me, too . . ."

2

Jim, Ted, and Craig and Deanna Humes arrived in Grand Junction early in the morning. After three unsuccessful days of searching, they had decided to sit down and approach the situation from another angle. Thus far, they had spent their time chasing down rumors, each of which had brought them great hope followed by greater disappointment. Jim had finally analyzed the available facts and information and decided it was time to take some very methodical, analytical steps to see if they were overlooking anything. The only concrete evidence to date was the ELT, which on Thursday had emitted a sort of strange dial tone. The CAP would be checking that out. But as they headed toward Monarch Aviation, they hoped to find something that would give them more direction or at least peace of mind.

Jim had already shared his own peaceful attitude with his friends on the way over. As a doctor he had seen patients die, and he had learned to accept the will of the Lord. He told his friends that if Sherleen was gone, the Jaussi family would be fine, because the Lord's will must come first. He wanted to take the trip to Grand Junction to clear up questions they each had in their minds, he said, but he wanted them all to start accepting the fact that Sherleen would not be coming home. The others found great comfort in his strength.

Jim and Craig decided that they knew enough about Sherleen and her patterns to tell that she had gone down quickly, with no time to radio. If there had been time or if she had decided to change her flight plan, she would have radioed and told someone. Because of this, plus the fact that a downed aircraft is usually found within twenty minutes of either its departure or arrival areas, they pinpointed the section designated as grid 122 as the most logical spot for her to have gone down. Now they wanted to listen to her tapes and talk to other pilots who might have seen her.

From the pilots' lounge, they contacted the CAP and learned that several planes were now flying over grid 122. In addition to the sporadic ELT signal coming from that direction, a pilot yesterday had spotted a flash (Sherleen's mirror!) and had flown over and over the spot but had not been able to pick it up again. In addition to the airplanes, helicopters were preparing to go up early that morning.

While they waited for word on what the helicopters found, Jim and the others talked to several persons who had seen and spoken with Sherleen on Tuesday. She had conversed with one pilot at length, spreading her maps out on the wing of the plane to make sure she understood each valley and mountain on her route. It was so like Sherleen to ask questions if she had any. The pilot had seen her leave with a right turnout, heading directly on course, and had watched her gain altitude until she was out of sight.

They also met and talked with flight service station chief Eric Wilstrom. He cleared up some of the rumors they had been hearing all week, and also related a couple of stories about some unusual turbulence on Tuesday.

The tower supervisor, Virgil Berridge, made an exception to the privacy act, which requires written consent from Denver, and allowed them to listen to the tapes of Sherleen's in-flight conversations. Grateful for his compassion, they sat and listened to the voice that for the past four days they had longed to hear—the voice that they wondered now if they would ever hear again. When they had listened to the entire transcription, they felt that they had finally found some of the answers and peace of mind they had sought all week. Gone were any questions Jim may have wrestled with as to Sherleen's ability to function that day as a pilot. Gone were the awful doubts Craig had had regarding Sherleen's preparedness. Her conversations with the tower were clear and organized, and her thoughts appeared to be totally collected. Her responses were immediate, and she appeared to be confident in everything she said.

A sense of relief settled on the little group huddled around the speaker. Sherleen had been calm and assured, negating the rumors they had heard during the week of panic, confusion, and lack of confidence. They knew that Sherleen would ask a lot of questions to make sure she had all the information she needed. To those who did not know her well, this may have given a mistaken impression. But through the conversations on the tapes and with various people at the airport, Jim learned that she had landed the plane perfectly, was within a minute of her estimated time, knew her heading and instruments, and had asked for help in interpreting her maps. These assurances settled a lot of Jim's questions, and he was quite relieved. But relief would not bring Sherleen back.

As they waited in the lounge for word from the helicopters, Jim visited with a pilot who had logged over 5,000 hours of instruction time.

"Have you ever been involved in a search?" Jim asked.

"Yes, I've been helping with searches for ten years."

"Have you ever found anyone you've been looking for?"

"Oh, no. Only once have I even been in the *vicinity* when someone was found."

Outwardly nonplussed, Jim continued, "Then—a search is really discouraging, isn't it?"

"Yes, it really is. But it has to be done." The pilot

echoed Ott Webb's sentiments—"It really makes us uncomfortable to leave an area because then we have to cross
it off and say 'he's not in that area.'"

Jim was still thinking about the conversation when
news about the helicopters arrived. They had returned to
Hill Air Force Base in Ogden, Utah, for the day. Discouraged, Deanna called Don Kent at the CAP and learned that
the choppers had found nothing. Perhaps they would try
again tomorrow.

The day had had some bright moments, but the fact
that the helicopters had come up empty cast a pall over
the group in the pilots' lounge. They had been so sure that
grid 122 was the right place to search! Together they cal-
culated again, and they were more sure than ever of Sherleen's position. She *had* to be in grid 122—she just couldn't
speak to them!

Jim finally agreed to a ground search, and he and Ted
decided that grid 122 was where the ground searchers
should concentrate. When he contacted CAP officials to
make sure that would be all right, he learned that that
area had been searched thoroughly from the air and they
were just about to give up on it. Even the ELT signal that
they had been trying to pinpoint for two days had now
faded.

"Then do you care if we bring in some people to
search from the ground?" Jim asked. "Will we interfere
with your search?" He was assured that the answer was no
on both counts.

Jim and his companions then went to the Bureau of
Land Management to get a map. Craig transferred grid
122 airspace to the land map. Next, each road was assigned a number, and the map was divided into eight sec-
tions, each a twenty-five-square-mile area. All that remained was to make copies for each of the vehicles that
would be going out in the morning.

The Cherokee landed in Price earlier than it had all week. Jim and Ted were anxious to meet with the men from the ward who would be participating in the ground search the next day.

The parting at the airport as Jim told the Humes of his feelings was a tearful one. "I want us to make this one last effort tomorrow, and then I want us all to accept the will of the Lord and know that things will be okay. I would like very much to bring her body back home, but I can accept that too if that is not to be." Deanna could no longer control the flood of emotion that gripped her. She sobbed violently. Craig was crying too, and grabbed Jim's arm in desperation as the sobs racked his frame.

"It's all right, it's all right," Jim said over and over to the couple. "It's all right."

3

For Sherleen, the day had begun on a hopeful note. At about eight o'clock in the morning, as she sat by a single quaking aspen at the edge of the clearing, she heard the search planes coming. Crawling out by the sagebrush, she frantically waved her makeshift flag and screamed at the three airplanes that one by one completely circled the clearing. *They've seen me!* she exulted. Treating herself to a celebration breakfast, she took out the last of the apple and relished everything but the seeds. Soon she'd be home, and she'd have real food again!

An airplane, of course, could not swoop down and pick her up, so she waited for a while. Hope and relief surged through her as she heard the unmistakable whirr of a helicopter. *This has got to be it.* But the helicopter never came in full view, and soon the chopper sound disappeared completely. *What problems could he have picking me up?* she wondered.

Some time later a yellow Jeep pulled up at the edge of the trees on the opposite side of the clearing. *They must have sent a ground vehicle to get me,* she reasoned. Again she waved and screamed. After a few moments the vehicle turned away, and she thought the driver probably couldn't figure out how to get over to her. Once again she waited, certain they would figure something out and reach her soon.

Why is it so hard to get me? I thought the hard part was finding me, but now that you know where I am, why haven't you come to get me?

All day she waited, but no one came. As the day wore on, the scorching heat drove her deeper and deeper back into the trees. During the long, hot afternoon the sound of an airplane sent her scurrying back to the clearing again, but it was only a plane crossing overhead on its own business, probably en route to Blanding. The yellow Jeep didn't return, and she finally surmised that the driver had probably been checking on cattle instead of looking for her. (Only later did she discover it had actually been a CAP vehicle!)

The sound of a kitten crying in the sagebrush nearby startled her. When the creature emerged from around a bush, it wasn't a kitten at all but a tiny fawn scarcely bigger than the Jaussi's dog, BoJo.

"Hello, how are you?" Sherleen greeted him, delighted to find a friend. But the fawn hurried off, as Sherleen called after it, "Oh, why don't you stay and keep me company?"

Alone again, she noticed some small strawberry plants. No berries were on them, but she chewed on some of the leaves. *If only I had just a bite of the apple left.* She tried eating the bark on one of the quaking aspens, but it was very bitter. More and more she felt as though her throat was closing shut, and she was now having trouble swallowing. She found the tube of hand cream in her purse and licked the lotion, which felt very soothing as it went down her throat.

With nothing to do, she looked again at the tree from which she had picked some bark. Then, using her thumbnail, she worked carefully to carve out a *J* in the trunk of the tree. It could have stood for "Jaussi." It could have represented the name of any of the children. But it wasn't any of those. This *J* stood for Jim.

4

At four in the afternoon, Sharon Madsen received word from her husband, Ted, that the ground search was on. She contacted Susan Lemon, and the two of them began calling everyone to verify, "They *are* going. Join us at the church for a meeting at six o'clock."

Most of the men planned to leave that evening and stay over in Grand Junction, so a lot of food was needed for that night as well as the next day. Food for the ground searchers had been accumulating at the Jaussi home all day, and Jean Jaussi and her daughter-in-law Sandy began portioning it into boxes for the searchers. They were amazed at how prepared the men would be, as they packed granola bars, canned meats, apples, oranges, bananas, nuts, cookies, peanut butter, candy bars, juices, and matches into each box.

The sheriff's department called Jim just as he arrived home from Grand Junction. News of the search had spread, and a deputy tried to convince Jim he should call it off. He was sure that a ground search would create more problems than it could possibly solve. Jim realized that the man was only doing his job, and that he certainly had reason to be concerned—it *did* seem hopeless. Jim's sister-in-law, Sandy Jaussi, who had been a member of the CAP herself, also tried to dissuade Jim. But Jim assured every-one who was trying to intervene that every possible safety precaution was being taken, that no children would be going with them, and that all the searchers would be out of the hills before dusk. He felt strongly that the search should proceed.

The entire Jaussi household, along with the families of the other men involved, went to the church at six to lend their support to the searchers. Though it was still quite light, the sun was no longer as brutally hot as it had been several hours earlier. Instead, it felt comforting to those who gathered in the parking lot. The bishop stood on the running board of one of the vehicles and called the meet-ing to order, then turned it over to Jim.

Jim's instructions to the group were very clear. He was determined to avoid further danger to anyone, and the search must be as orderly as possible. Only four-wheel-drive vehicles would be taken on the mountain roads, and each vehicle was to be equipped with food, water, emergency supplies, and a CB radio. He wanted the men to understand clearly how they were to search and what they were to look for. "We're going to look for her body, but I couldn't feel good about ending the search until we've made this last effort. No one is to take any un-necessary chances. Don't leave your vehicle and go off hik-ing alone. Stay together. Drive a thousand yards, get out and look as far as you can with your binoculars, then get back in and drive some more. Look for a wing, a piece of the tail, a wheel, any broken piece of the plane. If you see something you can't get at easily, radio for help, and we'll have the professionals brought in.

"Ward conference is to be held on Sunday, and I don't want anyone staying over to search after tomorrow night. We belong in ward conference. The Jaussi family will be in church together on Sunday, and we'll go forward together

61

and be fine." His voice faltered slightly, then he completed the instructions. "We want to turn this over to the Lord, put it in His hands. We must make it a spiritual journey so the Lord can lead us to her."

Susan Lemon took the map to make copies. The copies didn't turn out well, and she said as she distributed them, "The maps are not very clear. You will just have to be guided by the Spirit."

Jim went home for the night. He planned to fly to Grand Junction in the morning to join the rest of the searchers.

Throughout the evening the men departed in small groups, intending to get motel rooms in Grand Junction for the night and be ready to begin the search early the next morning. Lynn Lemon rode in a camper with Gardell Grundvig. Gardell had put a mattress in the back of the camper so that Sherleen could be comfortable once they found her. On their way out of town they ran into John Edison, who stopped his car and came over to talk to them.

"I sure wish I was going with you guys," he said. "I already made plans with my father to go on a fishing trip this weekend, and I really feel as though I'm committed to him."

"Don't worry about it, John," Lynn answered. "We have lots of people going, and I know some people already had plans. You couldn't help that. I know you'd come if you could."

"Are they going up again Sunday?" John asked. "I could come join you then."

"No, John, we won't be going Sunday. We won't need to go Sunday. We're going to find her tomorrow."

"I hope so, Lynn," John responded.

"Oh, we are."

"I hope so."

Grand Junction usually has plenty of motel rooms available in the winter, but this was summer, and the men from Price were surprised that every motel they tried was full. A convention was going on, and only one room could be found. Two or three of the men who hadn't brought sleeping bags along took that room, and the others decided to head out to the KOA campground. As Gardell Grundvig pulled out of the full lot at the Holiday Inn at eleven-thirty on his way to join the others at the campground, John Edison pulled up.

"Are you lost?" Lynn asked, surprised to see him there.

"No, I'd like to go with you and Gardell on the search."

John's boat had been all loaded and ready to go to the lake, but the more he talked about wanting to join the search, the more he knew that he must. His wife had finally said, "John, that's the Spirit telling you to go. You'd better do it." His father had understood completely. "If you're compelled to go, John, you've got to go."

5

Twenty miles directly southwest of the KOA campground, Sherleen slept. Steve Heidelberg, a counselor in the bishopric, came by with the girls in her Young Women's class. They were on their way to camp, and Sherleen was touched that they would stop and see her first. They left her there, knowing that she was all right, and continued on. They planned to pick her up on their way back when camp was over.

It was a lovely dream. The thunder and lightning that interrupted it didn't disappoint her, however, because she was eager to try to collect some rainwater. The rain did come, but the rainfall was light, and though she held her mouth open to get the moisture, probably no more than a drop went in. Sherleen was amazed that so many drops can fall—but none of them fell into her mouth. Even the cylinders she had planned to catch a drink in didn't get very wet, but she reached her fingers way in, trying to get out what she could. After the rain stopped, she licked the cardboard box, trying not to think about how it had been dragged over the ground.

She slept again, curling her feet up tightly in the box, hoping the dampness would not cause new problems. With her feet she felt her purse in the box. Inside the purse was her little white notebook, in which she had added more to her letter to Jim:

Well, another day has gone and I'm still here. It is 8:00. And here we were going to be in Provo tonight and S.L.C. tomorrow. I'm sorry, everyone. This is really a bummer—for all of us.

If I could walk, I have very seriously thought of walking out. Maybe it is just as well that I can't. I'd probably get lost. Worse than I am now, if that's possible.

I dread the night. I'll think of you all night and that will help it go by quickly.

Saturday, June 27

1

For the fifth time in as many days, Jim met Craig and Deanna Humes and Ted Madsen at the airport. This morning there was a different feeling from that of the previous days. They knew that today was the last day they would be searching together. Each day had brought a mood of its own, and today even Ted was less positive than he had been earlier. He arrived with his usual cheery smile but admitted, "Today has got to be a good day—I have no big plans or expectations."

Jim reflected on how much he appreciated the support and encouragement of Ted, Craig, and Deanna. They had given every ounce of energy and effort they could possibly muster over the past few days, and a bond had developed among them that they would each continue to cherish.

By the time the Cherokee landed in Grand Junction at

seven o'clock, the twenty-four other men were already at the airport for assignments and final instructions. Jim and Ted were happy to see their friends waiting for them, and the sight of all those volunteers so anxious to help Sherleen gave Craig and Deanna new hope.

Everyone gathered in the pilots' lounge of Monarch Aviation, where plans were finalized. Each person and vehicle was assigned a number to correspond with the areas into which grid 122 had been divided. Jim wanted to make sure that everyone was carefully accounted for both during the day and after the search was over that evening. He reiterated his firm desire that the search not interfere in any way with ward conference. "Those who need to go back for the meeting tonight, I want you to go back. *No one* is to stay over tonight. We want you to come back here to this room and sign out before you head for home, even if it's out of your way. Everyone must sign out here between 5:00 and 6:00 P.M. If anyone is still out after 6:30, let it be known that we're going to be coming out after you."

The volunteers discussed the rugged terrain they would be traveling through, and Jim reminded them again that they were to take no chances, but were to stay near the road and their vehicles. "We are going into an area that has been searched for days with airplanes, helicopters, electronic equipment, and some ground searching," he said. "The chance of finding her alive is nearly impossible, and even the odds of finding her body are slim."

The mood was solemn as he added, "All the armies in the world couldn't find Sherleen if she's not supposed to be found. But if she is, this group right here can do it."

Ted was emotional as he shared with the group a newspaper article he'd read three months earlier. It discussed the drought and what a serious situation it was becoming. The article had ended facetiously, "Don't worry, the Mormons are praying for rain!" The writer had taken a sarcastic jab at the faith of the Mormons, but it wasn't long before people began to wonder if the rain would ever stop. The spirit was strong as the group joined together in prayer before their search.

Only Craig and Deanna Humes remained as the ground searchers quickly cleared the room. They felt somewhat lonely as the enthusiastic volunteers disappeared one by one. Today they were not going to do any active searching, but there were still some leads and unresolved questions that had cropped up in conversations throughout the week. Deanna wanted to track them down on the telephone. She began by contacting the CAP, then all the little airports along Sherleen's route—at least ten in all.

2

Not many miles away, Sherleen crawled out to the clearing and announced to the sagebrush around her, "Well, here we go again with another day." She listened anxiously for the sound of airplane engines. The first sounds she had heard early that morning had been frightening ones, as two coyotes fought violently on the other side of the clearing. The noises had continued for over two hours, and she was certain one of the animals was dead by the time the sounds ceased. Now she was more anxious than ever to hear some comforting human sounds.

On almost the same schedule as yesterday, the planes came and circled the clearing above her. Sherleen waved frantically with one arm while with the other arm she waved the flag. So sure was she that she had been seen that she gave a friendly wave of appreciation to one of the pilots who seemed to be looking directly at her. All three planes flew just two or three hundred feet overhead, and once again she was positive that it was just a matter of time till they could get her out of there.

3

Jim, Brent Johnson, and Ted Madsen headed for their assigned area in Jim's Suburban. They wanted to check out some mountains and deep canyons south and east of Grand Junction that they had seen from the air that day and the day before. As they drew closer, they were dismayed to discover how many places couldn't be seen from the road that would have been visible from the air. Suddenly Ted, always the optimist, spotted something shiny across a canyon. Looking through his binoculars, he thought he could make out a wing—and not only was it a wing, there were numbers on it! Eager to investigate, he hiked across the canyon a mile and a half while Jim and Brent drove on and continued looking. When they returned a while later to pick him up, Ted had walked back to the road empty-handed and disappointed.

4

Gardell Grundvig, Lynn Lemon, and John Edison, who were assigned area number four, left the airport around eight-fifteen and headed toward the mountains. Thirty minutes later they were still driving around Grand Junction, crossing and recrossing river bridges and getting more confused by the minute. "How are we ever going to find her up in the mountains if we can't even get out of Grand Junction?" someone commented wryly. Finally, at about nine o'clock, they worked their way out of the maze, drove out of the city, and found the road toward their area.

Leaving the flat, green fields of Grand Junction behind them, they came rather suddenly to the Colorado National Monument. All at once they were surrounded by giant rocks jutting straight up out of the ground for one to two thousand feet. They shuddered to consider Sherleen's fate if she had gone down anywhere in that area. The Colorado National Monument is a magnificent statement of nature, a thrilling sight if one is not looking for a plane crash victim. The road through it winds for several miles, taking hairpin turns through huge, deep canyons, with thousand-foot cliffs and deep crevices all around.

At a ranger station in the roadway, the men stopped the truck, and paid their one-dollar fee to get into the park. Still confused about the map, they asked the ranger for help, but even with her directions, found it difficult to reach their assigned area.

Not only was it hard to find *where* they were supposed to go, but also *how* they would get there. They had diagrammed on the map what their general approach would be: starting at one corner of their small grid, they planned to move across, then down to the corner, working through the middle and back out the same way. But the first few roads they tried all had No Trespassing signs posted, with locks that had a length of pipe over them. John suggested that perhaps they ought to shoot the locks off, but finally they came to one road that was accessible. Not many feet in, however, they realized it would be impossible to drive on; crevices five feet deep blocked their way. Once again they searched for an access to their area. No road was available. At every turn they were met with either a dead end or a locked gate.

5

After they had been searching for a while, Brent said, "Jim, obviously you think Sherleen is not alive."

Jim looked at his companions. It was one thing to have reached that conclusion from overwhelming, inescapable fact, from the accumulation of years of medical experience. It was quite another to actually voice that conclusion to his friends. But Brent was looking at him expectantly.

"Medically it's impossible for her to still be alive," Jim said quietly. "Perhaps it's a kindness if she *is* dead. If she was hurt badly enough to be unable to reach help, she would be suffering immensely. I can't make myself want that."

Brent and Ted nodded.

Jim continued. "I want to find her body. Neither her mother nor I can stand the thought of leaving her out here."

Jim's quiet acceptance went a long way toward keeping the three men in command of the situation. He wanted very much for the search to be followed through to its conclusion carefully and effectively. It was important to everyone involved that they feel they had done everything possible.

Jim expressed his thoughts about a memorial service for Sherleen. "I've been thinking we should probably have three services—one in Price, one the following day in Salt Lake City in our old ward, and then one in Montpelier."

The three friends planned the services together as they bounced over the rugged back roads through their assigned area. Throughout the long day they discussed how Sherleen's loss would affect Jim and their children. Jim dreaded going through what he had seen his brother-in-law go through only a year earlier, but he knew he must prepare for it.

From the practical aspects—insurance policies, her clothing, housekeeping—to treasured remembrances, the conversation kept returning to Sherleen. The day's conversation was far from sober—the three friends laughed and joked about a lot of things—but always it came back to Sherleen.

"You know," Jim said, "I always had to have Sherleen explain the jokes to me after we'd come home from a party. I guess I just won't understand them anymore. And another thing—I don't know what I'll do about my clothes. Sherleen always matched things up for me."

Sherleen had always been Jim's navigator too—even in downtown Salt Lake City, where he had lived for so many years, he could still get lost.

Throughout the day Jim felt the sweet presence of the Spirit. He was sure it was because he had given himself up to the Lord's will.

Brent also found himself strengthened by his association with Jim and Ted during the day. As they turned to make one last search on the way back to Grand Junction, he remarked, "I wish Leila had been with us today. I've had such a special day, and I'm going to be able to accept Sherleen's death now. But Leila's not. I wish she could have heard and felt all the things that I've experienced."

6

Gardell, Lynn, and John still had not gained access into their area. At one point Gardell looked over in the trees and noticed something sheared off, such as an airplane might have done. The three men got out, walked down through the trees, saw some deer, and discovered a sawmill, but nothing else. They returned to the truck in about fifteen minutes.

"We're wasting time. We've got to get on the right course," Gardell declared.

"Let's pray again for help and direction. We can't afford to waste any more time going in false directions."

The three men climbed back into the truck and prayed. Then Gardell started up the motor again, and they continued on along a dirt road, coming to yet another locked gate directly in their path. While Lynn tried to unlock it, John began unraveling the fence next to it. Gardell looked carefully at the fence. Along it was something of a road—actually more like an overgrown path, obviously not traveled recently by any vehicle. He suggested they drive along the fence to see if they could find another opening, then turned the truck so he could move along the left side of the fence. A moment later he saw something off in the trees and asked, "Are those cows?"

"Yeah," John answered. "It's a bull and a couple of cows."

"Look, there's a sheepherder," Lynn joined in. "Maybe she's got the key to the gate. Let's ask her if she can help us get in."

John, who was nearest the window, thought he heard the woman call out, "Please help me." He turned to the others and asked, "Hey, guys, what do we do?"

"Well, let's ask her if she's got the key to that gate," Lynn suggested again.

They climbed out of the truck and called back, "Can we help you?"

"Yes. My leg's hurt. I can't walk."

The three men jumped over the fence and headed toward the woman. After a few steps, an incredulous John, who had taken the lead, called back, "Hey, I think this is Sherleen! It is! It's *Sherleen!*"

Quickly the three men converged on the tiny, frail woman who had come to mean so much to them. Each one wanted to take her in his arms, to hold her close and love her. One of them kissed her hand, and over and over the three of them chorused, "You're alive! You're really alive!"

Sherleen, drinking in the sight of the first faces she had seen in five days, laughed and exclaimed, "I can't believe I've been found! And I can't believe it was by someone I know! Have you guys got any water? I'm *so* thirsty!"

Lynn leaped back through the brush after the Thermos, and John and Gardell said, "Here, Sherleen, put your arms around our necks, and we'll help you back to the truck."

"Oh, please carry me, just carry me. I'm so dirty, and I know I smell terrible. But please carry me."

"No lady, you're not dirty, you're beautiful!" John said for the three of them.

"Make sure you get the purse with my letters in it!" Sherleen insisted as Gardell began carrying her. About halfway to the truck, Lynn met them with the Thermos and began pouring water down her throat, spilling it all over her.

"Oh, you're getting me all wet!" Sherleen choked, but Lynn answered, "It's all right, you're okay. You're alive!"

The three men couldn't get their fill of looking at her, touching her hand, trying to make her comfortable. Although her makeup had long since faded, the wedge-cut hairdo still fell obediently into place. Her pants and velour shirt had weathered the ordeal very well—a bloody knee in one pant leg and three drops of blood on the shirt, but not a single rip in either. Her strapped shoes were intact, as was her jacket. Her cheeks were a bit more sunken and her brown eyes somewhat gaunt. Her already thin frame seemed even more frail, but aside from being a bit wrung out and exhausted, Sherleen Jaussi looked wonderful.

While Lynn and Gardell made Sherleen comfortable on the mattress in the back of the truck, John got on the CB radio to inform everyone of the glorious news. No one answered! Quickly they turned the truck toward the general store they had seen about ten miles back, racing past the

Mudsprings campground, past Miracle Park, past cabins. Sherleen yelled, "We're going so fast! I'd hate to think I've lived through a plane crash only to die on the road now!"

Gardell *was* driving fast. The three men could hardly wait to share the wonderful news with her family and with the other men who were out looking for her.

Sherleen drank in the sight of the landscape speeding by, the feel of the mattress beneath her, the happy voices of the men who had found her. She was truly on her way home! How could she ever describe her feelings as the blue truck came to the same place where she'd seen the yellow truck the day before? *Someone's coming,* she thought. *Stand up, stand up!* The pain was intense, but she didn't care. She just knew that she had to stand up. So she had leaned against the tree to support herself, waved, and called.

Within minutes the truck pulled in at the store. Gardell and John ran inside to call the airport, while Lynn used the telephone outside to call the sheriff. He told him the frequency they had been using and asked him to inform the rest of the men that the search was over. Then he yelled at Sherleen, "What is your home phone number?" Quickly he dialed it. But the line was busy, so he called his own home, wanting to get the news to Sherleen's family as quickly as possible.

Susan Lemon had been trying all day to get away from the house and take care of some errands, but she hadn't yet made it. When Lynn's call came she knew why, and as soon as he yelled into the telephone, "Susan, Sherleen's okay! She's alive! Run over and tell her family!" she hung up the receiver and ran out the door. She drove as quickly as she dared, honking her horn as soon as she turned the corner onto Apple Circle.

When Lynn told Sherleen that her line was busy, she gave him Jim's private, unlisted number, and he dialed that. The operator said to Jean Jaussi, "I have a collect call from Lynn Lemon and Sherleen Jaussi."

Jean misunderstood and answered sadly, "Sherleen Jaussi is not here."

"No," Lynn interrupted, "you don't understand. It's not *for* Sherleen, it's *from* Sherleen!"

Nearly simultaneously Susan Lemon arrived at the Jaussi front porch and began pounding on the door. People gathered from all over the house, and eight-year-old Jean asked with wide eyes, "They found my mommy and she's okay?"

The house went wild. Jean hollered above the confusion, "I can't believe it! Is it really true?"

"It is! It really is!" Lynn shouted back.

"Then I'll most certainly accept the charges!"

Lynn carried Sherleen to the phone booth, and she stood, leaning against the walls of the booth. One by one the joyous voices of her family came over the line. The first wave of reality hit as she suddenly realized she felt hurt, tired, and ill. But she wanted to talk to them all.

She spoke first to Jim's mother and then her own. "Oh, Mother, I was so worried about you!" she said when Lola came on.

"Sherleen, this is the best news I've heard since you were born!"

Lynn stood back and watched, relishing every moment, as Sherleen talked with her family. In Price Susan Lemon left to share the news with Leila Johnson and the other neighbors. Someone at the door told her, "You know, your husband was one of those who found her!" Susan's eyes brimmed with tears. All week she and Lynn had felt so strongly that Sherleen would be all right. It had all happened as they had been impressed it would. Susan had seen Sherleen alive and well in a dream, and Lynn had seen her leaning against a tree as he prayed for her.

By the time Sherleen hung up the phone, the Jaussi house was alive with happiness. The tears of sorrow that had flowed all week turned to tears of joy and gratitude. The children got out paint and, with the neighbors' help, wrote welcome home messages all over the street. Others tied yellow ribbons to the branches of every tree in the cul-de-sac.

While the children decorated the yard and street, Jean Jaussi went with John and Sandy to the airport to thank the pilots and searchers who were still there. She shook hands with each one and expressed the gratitude of the entire family. Every face registered joy. Sherleen had been found and was alive!

7

Sherleen sat on the endgate of the truck, kicking her legs and sipping Sunny Delite citrus drink diluted with water. "I'll never again tell my children they're not really thirsty when they ask me for a drink!"

The sheriff arrived just ahead of the ambulance. He walked past Sherleen, asking, "Where's the victim?"

"I'm the one," Sherleen piped up from her perch.

"You're the victim?" he asked incredulously.

Sherleen didn't want to ride in the ambulance, but the sheriff told her she had no choice. She finally agreed, but she insisted that a friend ride with her; she'd been alone long enough.

After a hot, forty-five-minute ride to St. Mary's Hospital in Grand Junction, Sherleen was whisked into the hospital. Embarrassed at how dirty she was and that she had not been able to keep herself clean in any way during the week, she expressed her self-consciousness to the attendants.

"We don't care about that. We'll wash you and clean

you up and have you just lovely by the time your husband gets here."

A doctor came to examine her and determine the extent of her injuries. The cuts and bruises had already begun to heal nicely, but the "pulled muscle" inside the top of her leg turned out to be a broken pelvis, fractured in two places. Sherleen would never have been able to walk out of the Glade Park area where her plane had crashed.

The doctor started an IV. Sherleen insisted she didn't need it, but he was equally insistent. "Do you think after you've survived for five days in the mountains I'm going to let you die here in the emergency room because I let you talk me out of giving you an IV? My dear, you really have no idea how unstable you are!"

It was true. Sherleen felt wonderful. With every new arrival of a searcher at the hospital she relived the joy of being found.

8

Deanna and Craig Humes had been on the telephone at the Grand Junction airport, continuing their questioning of people at small airports in the area. In the middle of one conversation they heard the flight attendant say suddenly, "Just a minute—did you hear that? They found her—and she's alive!"

Deanna couldn't believe what she'd heard. She called the CAP for confirmation, and the people there were overjoyed to give it. Monarch Aviation rounded up a car for Deanna and Craig and had someone drive them to St. Mary's.

A lifetime had gone by since that early morning farewell five days before, and neither Craig nor Deanna had expected to see Sherleen alive again. They raced into the hospital, searching for her room. Then suddenly there she was, sitting in a bed in front of them. She looked wonderful—just as she had the day she left, except that Deanna was sure she could see a halo around Sherleen's head.

9

One more vehicle was still unaccounted for. All the others had arrived back at the airport by early afternoon, though some of the vehicles had just gotten into their assigned areas by the time the search was called off. But the last vehicle had gone way beyond the range of the two-way radios, and no one had been able to reach it. That vehicle was Jim's.

On their way back to Grand Junction, Jim, Brent, and Ted had stopped to check out a couple of more canyons. By the time they arrived at Monarch Aviation it was 6:15 P.M.

"Look at that," Brent exclaimed. "None of the four-wheel-drives are here."

"Looks as though they've all come in and gone home already. I'm kind of surprised that none of them stayed to talk to us." Jim felt a sense of abandonment.

They climbed wearily up the stairs to the pilots' lounge, which appeared to be deserted. Jim and Ted went over to the wall maps while Brent found the sign-out board and began signing them out, checking to see if everyone else was accounted for. Then suddenly he yelled, "Look at this! Russ Wilson wrote on the sign-out sheet 'Sherleen is found—go to St. Mary's Hospital'!"

A shot of electricity charged through the room. Jim, a pillar of strength all week long, began crying. Then the three men were pounding on each other's backs, jumping up and down, hugging one another. Suddenly Jim stopped and said, "That's a terrible joke to pull on me. Why would anyone do this?"

"Jim," Ted answered, "Russ Wilson would never pull a joke like this!"

As they scrambled down the stairs, Jim asked someone passing by, "Have you heard about it? Who found her?"

"A group from Price—from the church group that was looking," came the response. Jim began crying again. "The priesthood—the priesthood found her!"

For Jim, Sherleen had come back from the dead. He was in such a state of shock that Ted and Brent had to each take an arm and help him to the Suburban.

Somewhere on the way to the car they paused briefly and offered up a heartfelt prayer of thanks. Then they clambered into the Suburban, Ted asking, "Where's St. Mary's Hospital?"

Jim answered, "I think it's in Salt Lake."

Ted grinned at Jim's befuddlement and remembered there was a St. Mary's in Grand Junction. He asked directions from a woman inside the airport, and they were on their way.

Jim talked excitedly all the way to the hospital. "I don't care how she is—I'm a doctor, I can heal wounds. I can mend bones. I'll sit by her bed until she's better. I don't care *how* she is, as long as she's alive. I can't believe it!"

Every searcher had stayed at the hospital. They not only wanted to look at Sherleen, to be near her, but each of them was anxious for that priceless moment when Jim and Sherleen were reunited. Lynn Lemon was the first to see them arrive.

As Jim ran into the hospital he asked Lynn, "Who found her?"

"We did!" Lynn answered, and Jim wrapped his arms around Lynn and hugged him tightly. "I *knew* we were going to find her," Lynn added. "And if you'd had our area, *you* would have found her!"

Lynn led Jim down the hall to Sherleen's room for the big moment. She wasn't there! She had been wheeled down the hall to the phone, where she was being interviewed by an international press service from New York. Quickly Lynn and Jim ran to find her.

Sherleen looked up to see Jim rushing down the hall. She handed the phone to Brent and then Jim was beside her. Neither could find any words. Their eyes imparted much more than words as they drank in the sight of each other. Then Jim gently took her hand in both of his, kissed it, and gazed at the woman he loves.

Epilogue

The mood in the chapel at ward conference meeting that Saturday evening was a different one from that of the meeting held the previous Wednesday night. Jubilantly the congregation sang, "Now Let Us Rejoice." Then Bishop Crookston announced that the meeting would conclude early with a prayer by Brent Zollinger, one of the Jaussi family's home teachers, and they would adjourn to the airport.

The Cherokee touched down on the runway, then taxied around to allow those inside a view of the huge crowd that had gathered. Lola Hoskins finally dared breathe when she saw that Sherleen's face was as pure and unblemished as the day she had first been put into her arms.

As the door of the airplane opened and Sherleen came into full view, the crowd spontaneously joined in song, pouring out their love and affection in words that Sherleen already held dear to her heart—"I am a child of God, and He has sent me here . . ."

Brent Johnson, Bishop Crookston, and the others talked of the miracle. "We must expect to be better people now than before because we have been given much. Enjoying a spiritual feast or experience is not enough. There is a responsibility to *do* something, and not be hearers only."

The miracle blossomed. Sherleen had been found just in time. Saturday night torrential rains fell in the mountains around Grand Junction.

Deanna Humes spoke appreciatively of the pure, unquestioning faith of Jim Jaussi. "I hope I can always remember the strong desire I had to become like that myself, and never forget the spirit that surrounded us for five long days." Craig and Deanna did not forget. Six months after Sherleen's accident, Craig Humes was baptized. Both of them are now actively involved in the Church.

And on June 27, 1982, at 9:20 in the morning, exactly one year from the day her mother was found near the wreckage of her downed aircraft, Julie Jaussi was born.

Piper Tomahawk 2609-Delta after the crash

Kevin Mills/Sun Advocate

The J that Sherleen carved in a tree with her fingernail

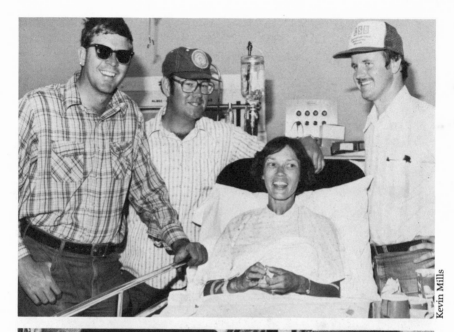

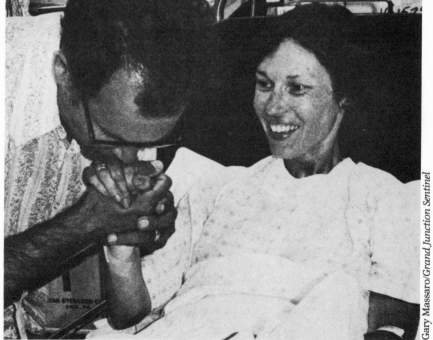

Sherleen with the three men who found her: Gardell Grundvig (left), John Edison, and Lynn Lemon

Jim Jaussi greets his wife for the first time after the rescue

Young James Jaussi helps decorate the street as part of a giant welcome-home message

*Judy Jaussi and Craig Crookston tie yellow ribbons to the
evergreens on the Jaussis' lawn*

Lola Hoskins (Sherleen's mother), Judy and Jean Jaussi, and a neighbor girl

Jan Jaussi (center) leads the rush to greet her mother at the airport

Steve Fidel

Steve Fidel

Judy and James Jaussi welcome their mother at the plane

Wendy Olsen (left), Jan Jaussi, and Craig Humes are all smiles at the airport

Steve Fidel

Sherleen (with microphone, center) talks to the crowd that gathered to celebrate on Monday, June 29, 1981